A Hightower Book

CHARLOTTE HUSKEY

authorHOUSE®

AuthorHouse™
1663 Liberty Drive
Bloomington, IN 47403
www.authorhouse.com
Phone: 1 (800) 839-8640

© 2017 Charlotte Huskey. All rights reserved.

Book cover by LouCindia Gellenbeck
Book artist, Rosi Gellenbeck

No part of this book may be reproduced, stored in a retrieval system, or transmitted by any means without the written permission of the author.

Published by AuthorHouse 05/16/2017

ISBN: 978-1-5246-8997-1 (sc)
ISBN: 978-1-5246-8995-7 (hc)
ISBN: 978-1-5246-8996-4 (e)

Library of Congress Control Number: 2017906616

Print information available on the last page.

This book is printed on acid-free paper.

Because of the dynamic nature of the Internet, any web addresses or links contained in this book may have changed since publication and may no longer be valid. The views expressed in this work are solely those of the author and do not necessarily reflect the views of the publisher, and the publisher hereby disclaims any responsibility for them.

All Scriptures are paraphrased or quoted from the King James Version of the Holy Bible.

Most song quotations are from Evening Light Songs published by
Faith Publishing House, Guthrie, OK, used by permission.

Churches and other noncommercial institutions may reproduce portions of this book without permission. When reproducing text from this book always, include the following credit line: "A Faithful Father Published by Charlotte Hightower Huskey, used by permission."

This book is available on Amazon and Christian book distributors worldwide.

Contact information:

E-mail: charlottenellhuskey@gmail.com
Facebook: Charlotte Huskey
Order by E-mail or phone 918-724-3613

This book is dedicated to Roberta (Hightower) Gaines
My sister, my friend and my teacher

Acknowledgments

A thousand thanks to Clifford Smith, Irma Sallee, Sandra Melot, and my daughters, Tricia Bell and Rosi Gellenbeck, for helping get this book into print. *A Faithful Father* would still be in manuscript form had it not been for their help.

Contents

Acknowledgments iv
Introduction vii
Characters in this book xi

Living in Oklahoma 1

1 Those First Years.. 1
2 Moving to a Farm 7
3 The Smokehouse Horse 14
4 No Bread for Breakfast 22
5 Where is Roberta? 29
6 A Summer with Grandma and Grandpa 34
7 Buried Alive! 43
8 Hit by a Speeding Car 49
9 Bringing in the Hay 55
10 God's a Good Mechanic 61
11 The Blizzard 67
12 Saying Goodbye to the Farm 73
13 A Year of Chaos 78
14 My Legs Don't Work 86
15 Does God Heal? 92
16 The Christmas Tree 98
17 The Stolen Candy 104
18 Spreading the Truth 111

Living in Oregon 117

19 A New Opportunity 117
20 Moving to Oregon 125
21 A New World 133
22 An 'Old Timer' House 140
23 A Little School, A Big House 148
24 Free at Last! 155
25 Tied in a Cherry Tree 160
26 The Day of the Fire 166
27 Silly Raccoons 172
28 Caught on The Train Bridge 178
29 A Ben Franklin Kite 185
30 A Lonesome Winter 191
31 A Letter from Uncle Cornelius 199
32 A Narrow Escape 204
33 Yellow Jackets at War 212
34 When Jimmy Ran Away 218
35 A Happy Daddy 225

Introduction

What does God expect of fathers? Is it to provide only material needs for his children? Does a father have the option to leave the care of his child to the mother or other caregivers? Did God design a place in a child's heart that only the father can fill? What is a father's duty?

The world, in general, expects more from a Christian father, but does not God require loyalty and compassion from all fathers toward this precious gift that he alone can give? Embracing this responsibility is not an easy job. One must struggle through sleepless nights, staggering hospital bills, temper tantrums, and embarrassing behavior. Anyone raising a family knows it is constantly necessary to make personal sacrifices for their children so that every child can become secure, mature, and emotionally stable. What a "heaven on earth" our world would be if every father accepted with enthusiasm his duty of leading his children.

Being a Christian father is much more than taking your sons and daughters to church, more than saying grace over meals, more than reading the Bible and praying with them, although all these are important. Don't we pray, "Thy kingdom come, thy will be done in earth as it is in heaven?" (Matthew 6:10) Are Christians given the option of pursuing personal dreams out of God's will? Aren't individual aspirations also to be committed to Him? Christ said, "Love one another as I have loved you." How did Jesus show love? He showed love by sacrificing himself, therefore, should we not sacrifice daily for one another within the family? If parents submit to God's will, He will put the Holy Spirit into our earthen body, enabling us to do His will as he did my father, Alvin. In this book, you will see Alvin keeping his faith steady and his family happy when material possessions were being stripped away. You will see Mabel making new flour sack dresses for her girls when she had only two dresses of her own.

I wrote this book to challenge and encourage fathers to make parenting their number one priority. I believe when the creator of life gives a child, it is the parents' responsibility to love that child as much as Jesus loves it. Jesus gave his life for every child and parents should likewise give themselves to the point of sacrificing a portion of our lives, especially during a child's early childhood.

I have woven my early childhood memories into the story because it is the story of an ordinary family. It is the account, like many others, of a family guided by a father who himself was struggling to know and do God's will. You might imagine Alvin as a kind of spiritual hero. He was human with human flaws. I hope it will inspire fathers to take up their God-given duties so that Proverbs 17:6, "The glory of children are their fathers," will be true as it was in my childhood.

I speak from experience. As a child, I saw God's love demonstrated through my father's actions. I never feared being abused, not even ignored, much less deserted. It has always been easy for me to trust God; because my father, through his devoted care for our family, proved to me that God is love.

If you are a father, ask God for strength, a desire, and grace to do your duty from this day forward. If you are a child reading this book, ask yourself this question, "Am I filling my God given roll within my family?" If you are a mother ask yourself, "Am I respecting and honoring my husband and fostering a positive joyful attitude in my children so they can face life's difficulties? By allowing the Holy Spirit to live through us, we can become parents that will bless our children with stability to be happy, responsible adults who hopefully will submit to God's will and also be successful parents.

Charlotte Huskey

Characters in this book:

Alvin Robert Hightower

Daddy

Lois May

Lois

Mabel May (Kelley) Hightower

Mama

Roberta Lee

Bob

James Pleasant

Jimmy

Charlotte Nell

Dink

Lou Ellen (Sharp) Hightower   James Alexander Hightower
Grandma   Grandpa

Cornelius Hall Hightower
Uncle Cornelius

Living in Oklahoma

1 Those First Years

...Be content with such things as ye have: for he hath said, I will never leave thee, nor forsake thee. So that we may boldly say, The Lord is my helper, and I will not fear... Hebrew 13:5b, 6

Mabel awoke to a loving kiss. She gazed into Alvin's soft blue eyes as he whispered tenderly, "Honey, I better be off, the day is beginning to dawn and I need to get the vegetables picked and taken to the farmer's market before it opens at six this morning. Don't worry about my breakfast, your body needs some extra sleep. For breakfast, I'll drop by Mom's or buy something at the market; however, I will be home to eat lunch with my wonderful wife."

Mabel's heart felt full and happy to be the receiver of his sacrifice and care. Her dream had become a reality! She had love, companionship, and family, things she had yearned for the most since her parents and siblings had been snatched away one by one.

Her mind flew back six years, to that cool September day when she stood in the cemetery beside her beloved papa's casket. She was alone and frightened, without a family member to cry with her, to share her sweet memories, to help pay for the funeral expenses, or to help her choose a stone to mark the grave where dear Papa lay. That day, Alvin had drawn close and supported her arm as her trembling legs walked away from her last family member. Mabel shivered at the thought of living alone in the apartment that she and Papa had shared, but Alvin had not let her feel alone. He started coming to see her every day, and her life began to bloom into a happy secure world. Within a few weeks he had proposed, and they were married a month later.

Mabel crawled out of bed dutifully because she wanted to do her household chores while Alvin was out doing his duties. As usual, she started her day with worship. "Dear Jesus, after all those years struggling alone and then caring for Papa, you have given me my heart's desire: a loving husband, three beautiful children and a home to keep. Thank you, Jesus. Please bless Alvin with good sales for his vegetables, and help me to be the best wife and mother that I can be. Amen."

She opened her Bible to Proverbs 31 and read what King Lemuel's mother had taught him about a good wife. Mabel read the chapter slowly, paying attention to every phrase, and again she prayed: "Lord, please help me to be a woman like the king described: one that is virtuous, trustworthy, supportive, and a diligent worker. Dear Jesus, also make me organized, capable in business, charitable, and fearless. Amen."

By now her children were waking up. Roberta, the youngest girl, woke up first as was her usual habit. Mabel pulled her up on her lap, brushed her curly, sandy-red hair back from her face and showered her with kisses. Soon Jimmy, her oldest, was up and then Lois followed him. She hugged and kissed each one as she got them ready for the day. I am so happy I feel that my heart could burst, she thought. She sang while preparing her children's breakfast.

When Alvin came in for lunch, Mabel noticed a long solemn look on his face. "You look worried," Mabel remarked. "Come, I have some potato soup and hot cornbread ready for you. Did things not go well today?"

"I will tell you about it later. I don't want to think about it right now," he whispered as he kissed her. Then he sat down with the children at the table.

After Alvin thanked God for the food, Mabel said, "We have had a good day. Thank you for working hard to provide for us. I am so happy to be staying home with our children."

"Oh, Mabel, I wish I could supply more. I waited until I was thirty-eight-years old to get married because I feared I could not provide for a wife and children and also help my parents. I knew I had to help them since Dad's heart is weak."

"So many banks went broke the same year we married and caused a plunge in our country's economy. It has made earning a living arduous for everyone. Yet, we have never gone to bed hungry," Mabel said.

"Yes, God has supplied our needs over and over again. I love tending the gardens and watching my vegetables grow; but people can hardly afford to buy what I have for sale. Well, I'd best be going. I've a lot to do before dark," he said, while he quickly finished eating his soup and cornbread.

"I wish I were able to help you."

"You need to rest, dear" he said, as he gave her a big hug and patted her bulging belly. "What shall we do when the baby decides to come?"

"Your mother asked us to stay at their house."

"So we'll plan on staying a few days at Mom's?"

"Dear, your mom is old fashioned; she thinks I need help for a whole month," Mabel answered.

"Then should we move our things out and let Mrs. Webber take her house back?" Alvin questioned. "I was hoping we could keep it. I saw her the other day and asked for another month's grace. And you can't believe how hateful she acted. She said, 'No, if you aren't out the last day of this month, I'll have you put out onto the street.' Then I mentioned that we were expecting a baby any day, so she softened and said we could stay another month."

"Let's not move anything. Maybe within a month God will work something out so we can keep our home," she said hopefully.

That night after the children were asleep, Alvin said, "I was sad when I came home for lunch, because I heard that the Lane family lost a whole year's earnings. You know, I've wished ever since we got married that we had been putting money in the bank to buy a farm. However, after hearing what happened to them, and knowing that many others lost all their savings too, it makes me know God is still in control and there was a reason he didn't allow us to save at this time. Mrs. Lane hurried to the bank just before it closed and deposited $1,200. The bank closed that night. They lost it all, except for $5.00 that she had kept for groceries. I think God knows I couldn't have handled such a loss. It might have destroyed my faith."

"Alvin, don't ever let anything destroy your faith."

"I almost lost my faith in 1921. Dad bought land from the school and he, the three boys, and I worked day after day all through the long hot summer raising cotton. In the fall, when we were ready to pick it, the price of cotton went down to five cents a pound. We just left the cotton on the stalk in the field. We had already farmed two years and made very little profit, and that year was a complete loss. The boys went back to school, Dad bought a team of horses, and he and I went to work helping build roads for a few months until the ice and snow stopped the work. I then went to work at Wilson's Meat Packing House where you and I worked before we were married. In those years it was easy to find work. Now it's almost impossible to get any work that pays a decent wage. Why, I dug a long ditch for a woman the other day and she offered me only fifty cents. I just walked away disheartened."

"Oh, how terrible! But don't give up, *God will never leave us nor forsake us,*" Mabel said.

"I know, but sometimes it seems like He has forsaken us," Alvin answered.

"Alvin, God has helped you to make payments on this house, on Papa's funeral bill, and all the while keeping your family with necessary food and clothing."

"I guess it could be worse, but you have only one dress. Do you call one dress necessary clothing? Oh, Mabel—" Alvin remarked and laughed.

Mabel hugged him and said, "It's alright, you are doing the best you can. Things could be worse."

They did get worse.

Alvin's brother, Cornelius, was renting a house and the landlord forced him out. His wife's people had no place for him and his wife, their five children and a new baby, so they moved in with Grandma and Grandpa Hightower.

When Mabel heard about it, she exclaimed. "Oh! Alvin, I think I had better stay right here when the baby comes. I couldn't rest in a four-room house with ten children and seven adults living in it."

"But we have less than a month."

"We will make out somehow," Mabel agreed.

"We have always said, 'Working together and trusting in God, we can conquer any problem,'" Alvin reminded her.

"Yes, we can! Romans 10:11 says, *Whosoever, believeth on him shall not be ashamed,*" Mabel said.

Everyday Mabel and Alvin hoped the new baby would arrive before they had to move. Every morning Alvin tried to sell his carrots, tomatoes, sweet potatoes and onions he had grown. In the afternoons he walked the streets of Oklahoma City searching for jobs to earn money to pay the three delinquent house payments. He walked until his shoe soles wore thin. He put cardboard inside his shoes to protect his feet from the burning sidewalks. Every evening they prayed for a miracle from God. Every day was the same hot weather, hard work, scant pay, worry, fear of the future, until even Mabel's faith was stretched thin.

Then the day came when they had to give the key back to Mrs. Webber, and the new baby hadn't arrived. With tears streaming down her cheeks, Mabel packed Alvin's and the children's few clothes into her old trunk on top of her keepsakes. Alvin mechanically loaded their beds, table and chairs into Uncle Ezra's little pickup. He threw in a wash tub of pans and tin dishes, then his few tools and headed for his mother's home on South Shield Street in Oklahoma City.

Questions for discussion:

1. Why did Alvin get up early?
2. What did he do that showed his love?
3. Who changed Mabel's sad life into a happy one?
4. How did Mabel show her love?
5. Why did Alvin almost lose his faith?
6. Where did they go to live when they lost their home?
7. Have you been tempted to doubt God?

2 Moving to a Farm

. . . [He] is able to do exceeding abundantly above all that we ask or think, according to the power that works in us, Ephesians 3:20

Grandma's boarders also had lost their jobs and had moved away. Alvin and Mabel moved into Grandpa's little one-room house where the men had been sleeping. On the twenty-fifth of August, soon after they settled into the tiny house, a baby girl was born.

There was little quiet time or peace of mind for Mabel to recuperate after giving birth. The hot August sun beat down on the tiny house crammed with beds, a table, chairs and a two-burner cooking stove. Mabel's three toddlers had to play outside unsupervised with Grandma's other five grandchildren. Their cousin's mother had given birth to a boy just months before and she wasn't well.

Alvin left home early every morning seeking a bit of work here and there to buy a scant meal for his family. One day in his search for a job, Mr. Broady offered him something too good to be true.

Alvin hurried home with Mr. Broady to talk with Mabel. She met them at the door with baby Charlotte in her arms.

"Mabel, this is Mr. Broady. And this is my wife, Mabel."

"Come in and have a seat," Mabel said.

"Glad to meet you, Mrs. Hightower," Mr. Broady said politely. "What a beautiful child. What's the name?"

"Her name is Charlotte, but we've been calling her Dink. She's the smallest of the 10 grandchildren running around here. It's great to meet you too, for I've heard the family speak highly of you."

As soon as the men were seated, Alvin began talking excitedly. "Mr. Broady has a farm seven miles out of town with a good house, and he is looking for someone to live there and farm the land." Then turning to Mr. Broady, Alvin added, "Maybe you should explain it to Mabel."

Mr. Broady began to explain: "Well, I've had problems with my wife and she's gone and divorced me. I have a farm east of the city with animals, a cow, horses, and chickens. My work keeps me away a lot of the time; therefore, I need someone to live in the house and take care of things. I've known Alvin's family a long time and know they are honest hardworking people who will do right by me. So when I saw Alvin in town today I told him about needing someone to care for the farm. Think you might be interested in living out there?"

"Don't you think that would be good for us?" Alvin interjected.

"Yes, I believe this is an answer to our prayers. We have been praying for another place to live. A farm would be perfect," Mabel answered.

"Then it's a deal! Wife has already moved her things out. You can move in any time."

"Is there a school near?" Mabel asked. "Our son, Jimmy, will be in the first grade."

"Yes, Soldier Creek grade school is near the farm," Mr. Broady answered.

Alvin cleared his throat and said, "Mr. Broady, I thank you for this offer. I believe this is the opportunity we've been wanting."

"Well, I have some business to tend to in town so I better go. Goodbye, Mrs. Hightower," Mr. Broady said as he smiled and did a little curtsy-bow of respect.

As soon as Mabel was stronger, Alvin borrowed his brother Ezra's truck. The early morning sun reflecting off the tree limbs looked like jewels of gold to Alvin. He hummed his favorite song, "Oh Happy Day," as he was getting the truck ready for moving.

Mabel sang "Jesus has been so good to me, no other friend so kind could be," as she was packing their few belongings. She packed her washtub full of dishes, cooking utensils, dish towels, rags, etc. She covered them tightly with her only tablecloth. Papa's old trunk, which Mabel and Papa had used in their many relocations to different cities, was already partially filled. Papa's lamp, his two shirts, Mabel's cup that had been given to her just before her mother died, her little toy iron and other keepsakes were in the bottom of the trunk. Mabel picked up Papa's picture and kissed it. She replaced the precious picture in its original box and stood the box carefully against the trunk wall. As she was packing, she was speaking with her friend, Jesus. "You know I am still missing Papa, although he has been with our family in heaven for seven years now. Only I, and I hope my brother Albert, are still on earth. Please keep Albert safe, and help me find him. And Lord, my heart is bursting with gratitude that you have given us a home in the country. Thank you!"

Mabel pressed down the things already in the trunk and added Jimmy's winter coat, his new overalls for school, the children's Sunday clothes, Lois' cap, coat and mittens, and Alvin's clothes. Sheets and pillow cases she had made from white flour sacks were folded and slipped into a clean sack. Then she filled a clean flour sack with underclothes and their two towels. She rolled up the patch-work quilts, tied them with string, and slipped them also into clean flour sacks.

When all was organized, Alvin took the wooden bed frames apart and stacked them in the bottom of the truck. Then he and Mabel lifted the heavy trunk and the washtub of dishes. Mabel emptied the corn shucks from the two bed ticks and rolled them into a bundle. They loaded their table and chairs, then tucked in the flour sacks full of quilts, sheets and clothes. Last of all, Alvin laid his pick, shovel, rake, hoe, and other heavy things on top to keep things from rolling out while traveling.

They said goodbye to everyone in the family. Grandma took each one in her arms and squeezed them tightly, for it might be months before she would see them again. She gave a special long hug to Lois. Grandma felt sorry for Lois because her little sister, Roberta, was born only 11 months after Lois. Grandma thought Lois didn't get to be a baby long enough. Grandpa took Roberta in his arms and rubbed his stickery whiskers all over her face until it turned pink. Roberta liked for Grandpa to "ruff her up" as he called it. Aunt Montella and cousins, Bill and baby Tom, hugged everyone, too. Their other cousins, Betty Lou, Ellen, Pete, and Kathrine were away at school.

Alvin and Cornelius had both lost their jobs and their homes after the big bank in downtown Oklahoma City closed down. They and their families were living at Grandpa Hightower's place– Alvin, in the little house in the back yard, and Cornelius and his family of eight lived with Grandma, Grandpa, and Uncle Ezra in the front house. On warm days, the children played outside together in the evenings until dark. On cold evenings, they sat around on the floor of the living room and listened to the three brothers and Grandpa tell stories of their childhood adventures.

After all the good-byes were said, Alvin helped Mabel with the baby into the front seat of the truck he had borrowed. Then he took baby Charlotte from her arms while Roberta scrambled up and found her place on Mabel's lap. With her situated, Alvin put Lois and Jimmy in and placed the baby in Jimmy's arms. "Hold her tightly, for she is a livewire and may try to wiggle out of your arms," Mabel cautioned Jimmy. Alvin jumped in and they headed for their new home on Broady's farm.

As they left Grandma's house, they drove past block after block of houses. They drove past shops, stores, car dealerships, the many tall hotels, and the big bank. Many businesses had "CLOSED" signs hanging on their doors. "There is the bank that went broke, causing so many men to be out of work and many families to lose their homes," Alvin told Mabel. They passed several rows of apartment houses, and then there were no more houses. It was just a long straight road. Here and there they passed a few farm houses. When Alvin came to a store, he slowed down and turned right onto a lane that took them up to their new home.

"Wow!" Mabel said, as she gazed on the beautiful farm. When she got out of the truck, she looked up toward heaven, opened her arms as wide as she could, and exclaimed, "Thank you God for this beautiful home!" Then turning to Alvin, she said, "Oh, Alvin, God has done more for us than what we asked. Look at this huge parcel of land for you to grow vegetables!"

"Yes, and there are horses waiting to help me prepare the soil, a big barn, a chicken house with chickens, and a shed for my car with room enough to keep our wood dry. We never thought to ask for all this," Alvin responded with a big smile. "It's like having our own farm without having to pay the payments."

Lois patted Mabel's arm, and pointing to the cow, she said, "Look Mama, a cow, and over there is a play house."

"That is a smokehouse," Mabel explained. "We can raise a pig and smoke our meat in the smokehouse and it will stay good to eat for a long time."

"We'll have milk to drink?" Jimmy asked, as Alvin and Roberta walked into the house.

Mabel nodded her head, yes.

The house had one big long room with a kitchen at the end and two smaller rooms. Mr. Broady had his things in one room, but the other would make a nice bedroom for Mabel and Alvin. "This room is so big it will work well for a dining room, living room and a space to put a bed for the children too," Mabel said. "And there is a nice corner here for me to wash clothes inside when the weather is cold. And look here, a lovely cook stove. This is much more than I expected."

As they began bringing their belongings inside, Alvin said, "I thank the Lord for this blessing. This winter may be rough; but by working hard and trusting God to bless the crops, we will have plenty to eat and vegetables to sell this coming summer."

Questions for discussion:

1. Why was Alvin's family living with his parents?
2. How many families were living there?
3. Name Alvin and Mabel's children.
4. How did God answer Mabel and Alvin's prayers?
5. What did Mr. Broady offer?
6. Why were many people without jobs?

Jimmy age five, 1935

3 The Smokehouse Horse

Thou will keep him in perfect peace, whose mind is stayed on thee: because he trusts in thee. Isaiah 26:3

The September day was warm. The girls were playing in the smokehouse. Jimmy was in school. Mabel was washing clothes as she did every day. Jimmy had only one decent pair of overalls for school. The girls had only a few changes and Mabel herself had only one dress. After hanging the clean clothes on the line, Mabel took the girls into the woods to explore while she looked for late producing wild fruit. She found a few small late peaches and ground cherries. These she placed into her basket. Everywhere, dusky-yellow persimmons were hanging on the trees. "Persimmons are not good to eat until after cold frosty days," Mabel told the girls.

"I want to taste one now," Lois said. Quickly, she pulled a persimmon from a tree and bit into it. "Yucky," she complained and spit it out.

"Now do you believe that they are not good?"

Lois nodded.

"Here is a beautiful creamy yellow fruit. We will ask your Daddy if it is safe to eat?" she said as she placed it into her basket.

Not far away she found orange-yellow fruit hanging underneath a vine. There were many so Mabel opened one. It was full of black seeds. She placed several in her basket. Along the fence she found what looked like small grapes. "Let's take these also and ask your Daddy about them."

"Look Daddy, we found fruit," Bob called when they got near where he was cutting wood. "Mama says you will tell us which ones are good to eat."

Daddy laid down his ax and knelt beside the basket. "This is a Paw Paw." He held up the pretty yellow fruit. "They are delicious. But I am surprised you found a tree. These usually grow in the Eastern part of this country. The orange-yellow ones with the black seed are passion fruit. These were originally a tropical fruit, but some have adjusted themselves to this colder climate."

"Are they good?" Bob asked, looking into Daddy's face.

"Taste it," he said, and held it to her lips.

"Me too," Charlotte said. And he gave her some. "Yum, yum."

"These wild grapes are mixed together with porcelain berries. You'd best throw them all away. Porcelain berries will make a person deathly sick." Daddy warned.

"How can we tell which are grapes?" Mabel asked.

"You must look at the vine's leaves. The grape leaf looks like this; and with his finger, he drew a grape leaf in the dirt beside his foot. The porcelain berry leaf looks like this. He drew another leaf. "Do you see the difference?"

"Yes, I do," Mabel said. "Now I will know which ones to pick."

"And we found a big tall tree with little nuts all over it," Lois said.

"That was probably a hackberry tree. The berries are good all winter. When I was a boy, we let our pigs run in the woods, and they found plenty of fallen hackberries."

"Can we eat hackberries?" Lois asked.

"Yes. They are kind of like a nut with a little sweet kernel in the middle that taste somewhat like a date," Alvin answered. "Some people call a hackberry tree a sugar tree, probably because the fruit is very sweet."

Mabel boiled the ground cherries and peaches with sugar. Then she mashed the fruit and drained it in a colander. It was enough to make fruit syrup for supper. She served the syrup over big round pancakes.

"Our fall garden is growing fast," Daddy said one evening as they were eating supper. "The barn will protect it from the cold north wind. The turnips, mustard, beets, green onions and spicy radishes will soon be large enough to eat; and if the weather isn't extremely cold, they will produce most of the winter. There is nothing better than a dish of turnip greens and cornbread on a cold winter day," he added.

"Not as good as syrup and pancakes," Jimmy answered with syrup dripping from the corner of his mouth.

"You made syrup with the wild fruit?" Alvin asked.

"Yes, and I threw the porcelain berries and grapes away. I'll look for more grapes now that I know how to identify a grape vine by its leaves. Maybe we will have grape jelly for our pancakes and biscuits this winter."

"You are like the woman described in Proverbs 31: dependable, diligent worker and fearless," Alvin remarked and smiled at Mabel. "Come spring there will be sand plums, mulberries, dewberries and wild greens."

"Oh yes, I sometimes gathered curly dock, lamb's quarter and poke weed for Papa. He said that they cleaned the body, and he always felt better when he had greens to eat. Maybe I could find some now."

Every few days Mabel took the girls and went hunting wild, edible food. She tramped through tall grass and brush to find only a handfull of greens and a few little fruits, however, it was enough to add flavor to their meals.

One day, very tired after returning from the woods, she lay down with the girls and went to sleep. When Jimmy came home from school, Dink was on the smokehouse. "Mama! Mama!" he called, as he opened the kitchen door, "Dink is sitting on top of the smokehouse!"

Mabel, half asleep, came running to the door. She shaded her eyes to be able to see in the bright sunlight. There across the yard she saw Dink on the roof. Mabel threw her hands into the air. "That child is bound to die before she's grown," she said. "Jimmy, see if you can get her down."

"Where is Mr. Broady?" Jimmy asked.

"He drove away before we took our nap," Mabel answered.

Jimmy climbed up onto the roof. He worked his way across the roof and pulled on Dink's arm. She kicked and screamed. "No. My hossey. Me wide hossey."

"You gotta come down," Jimmy said. "Mama said so."

"No," she yelled and hit at Jimmy as he pulled on her. "You wide Blackie, me wide me hossey."

By now Mama was beside the smokehouse with arms extended to catch Dink. After a long hard struggle, Jimmy got her down into Mama's hands. Mama took her into the house and followed instructions from *Proverbs 22:15. Foolishness is bound in the heart of a child, but the rod of correction will drive it far from him.* "It is very foolish for a two-year-old to climb onto a smokehouse," she reprimanded Dink, while heating up her behind. Her wailing awoke Bob and Lois. Jimmy told them what their wild little sister had done.

That evening when Daddy came in, they told him about Dink's foolish stunt. Daddy raised Dink above his head and said, "I declare, Dink, can't you tell the difference between a house and a horse? But listen little livewire, if you climb it again, you will also get some Proverbs from me. You understand?"

Dink nodded, "Yes."

Daddy was tired, he had been splitting wood all day. As soon as supper dishes were washed, he called the children together for family worship. The children hurried to get seated so they could choose their favorite songs. First, they sang one of Daddy's favorites songs. It was written by B. E. Warren.

"Tarry with Me"

Now the shadows slowly lengthen,
Soon the evening time will come;
With thy grace, O Savior strengthen
By thy help I would go home.

Tarry with me, O my Savior,
Tarry with me through the night;
I am lonely, Lord without thee,
Tarry with me through the night.

After all the songs had been sung, Roberta again climbed upon her soft straw bed to hear Daddy read the Bible. He opened the Bible, put on his glasses and read Isaiah, chapter 26:

In that day shall this song be sung in the land of Judah; We have a strong city; salvation will God appoint for walls and bulwarks. Open ye the gates, that the righteous nation which keepeth the truth may enter in. Thou wilt keep him in perfect peace, whose mind is stayed on thee: because he trusteth in thee. Trust ye in the Lord forever: for in the Lord Jehovah is everlasting strength:

Alvin took off his glasses and laid them on the Bible in his lap. Then looking over at Mama, he said, "Mabel, Jehovah God is our strength. As we keep our mind on him, He will keep us in perfect peace."

"I know, Alvin, He will never leave nor forsake us. God opened up this farm for us. We came without money or food and God is supplying all we need."

"Yes, working together and trusting God is what we must continue to do. He will see us through the winter. Thankfully we have plenty of wood to keep us warm and I have much of it split into the sizes that we need for the two stoves. If we have good crops this summer, I will be able to buy warm coats and boots for our family and store away food so we will be better prepared for next winter," Alvin said.

"Jimmy has a warm coat for school and the girls and I can stay inside on cold days," Mabel said.

After the children were sleeping and Alvin and Mabel were sitting by the fire, he said, "I'm so sorry I haven't been able to supply better for you and the children."

"I know you are doing the best you can, and I believe life will be easier this coming year. There were times I thought Charlotte was starving to death. But she is full of life. And now we have milk from the cow, eggs from the chickens, and hope of vegetables from our fall garden," Mabel said.

"You are such a positive woman! We have almost nothing and you are thinking only of the good that we have."

Mabel smiled and laid her head on Alvin's shoulder. They sat quietly for a while and then Mabel whispered, "I hate to tell you this, but I used all our flour making bread for supper."

Alvin put his head in his hands and groaned, "Oh, Lord, please help us."

"God will help us," Mabel said in a voice full of confidence. "Although our country fell into a recession the year we married, God has helped you supply for us these eight years. He won't fail you now."

"I know He won't," Alvin said with renewed determination.

Questions for discussion:

1. What fruit did Mabel find on the farm?
2. What did she make with the peaches and cherries?
3. Who will God keep in perfect peace?
4. Who kept Dink from falling?
5. Were they confident that God would supply?
6. How many years had God supplied for them?
7. Has God supplied something you needed?

Every evening before going to bed, the Hightower family sang together, read a portion of the Bible, thanked God for their blessings, and prayed that He would supply their needs.

4 No Bread for Breakfast

My God shall supply all your needs according to his riches in glory. Philippians 4:19

Alvin got up early. He built a fire in the stove and knelt beside it and prayed, "What can I do to get flour for bread? Show me Lord where I can earn some money."

Alvin was a farmer at heart. Farmers are people who prepare for winter by storing food. But this year he had barely been able to supply for the daily needs of his family. Now winter was staring him in the face and no food in storage, not even enough for breakfast. He was thankful to have a cow for milk and chickens laying eggs. But what about bread? "Lord you have never forsaken us, please don't let us down now. Show me, Lord, if there are hidden sins in my life that would keep you from answering my prayer. Clean me of any secret sins. Purify my heart so that my prayers will ascend to your holy throne. My family will be hungry today if you do not answer my plea for flour."

After prayer, he went out to milk the cow. As he was sitting on his milk stool, he heard his brother, Cornelius, say, "Good morning, Alvin."

Alvin looked up quickly at Cornelius. "What brings you here so early? And why are you huffing and puffing? Did you walk all the way from town?"

"Yes, I walked all the way from home," Cornelius said in between long hard breaths. "But listen, I have great news. Mr. Hunter has a fifty-pound sack of flour for us. He sent word by his wife, who told Mom when they met for prayer meeting last night. I've come to see if maybe you could go get the flour. The Hunters live way out—"

"And what if I have no gas in my car?" Alvin said teasingly, "You would be walking seven miles for nothing. No, not seven miles but fourteen miles, because you would also have to walk the seven miles back home."

"That's right, but you know a real man will walk many a mile to keep his children from being hungry. I couldn't watch my children go to bed hungry if I hadn't done everything in my power to keep it from happening."

"That is the way I feel too, and yes, I do have gas and I'll be more than glad to take you in my car to get the flour."

"Get a sack if you have an empty one, and I will share it with you."

"Mabel used all our flour making bread for supper last night. You came just in time to help us, too. Won't you go in and rest a few minutes while I take care of the cow and get the car ready?"

Still breathing hard, Cornelius said, "I do need a drink of water." He went into the house.

"Thank you, Lord, for supplying our needs," Alvin prayed, as he sat down to finish milking the cow. He put her back into the pasture. Then he filled the radiator of his 1926 Reo car with water and pumped up a tire that looked a little flat. He cranked the motor, and it started on the first crank.

Alvin went in and explained everything to Mabel. She clapped her hands and said, "Thank you, Jesus."

Then Alvin added excitedly, "Lord willing I should be back in a couple hours and you can make bread for breakfast."

After the men had gone, Mabel went into her bedroom and knelt beside her bed. "Thank you, Jesus, for providing flour for Cornelius and us. You are marvelous! I praise you for always taking care of our needs. And Jesus, I don't want to be selfish, but could you please supply some lard? My bread has been hard. Some fat would make it softer and much better." After praying, Mabel thought of trading the red hot peppers she had for some lard.

She called to Jimmy who was sleeping, "I want you to take these peppers to the store and see if Mr. Hilton will trade them for some lard."

"Can I ride Blackie?" he asked.

"Yes, just be careful. You could hurt yourself if you fall off. He's a big horse. It's a long way to the ground when you are on top of old Blackie."

"I'll be careful," Jimmy answered. He jumped out of bed, dressed quickly, slipped on his winter coat and ran out to the pasture.

While Jimmy went for Blackie, Mabel wrote a note.

Dear Mr. Hilton,

We are without money right now as many people are. If you think you could sell these hot peppers, would you please give me some lard in exchange for them?
Mrs. Mabel Hightower.

"Blackie, Blackie," Jimmy called. Blackie twitched his head and came running. He loved Jimmy.

Blackie stood beside the wooden gate so Jimmy could climb onto his back. Jimmy climbed up the boards of the gate, stood on the post and slid over onto the horse's back. However, he had forgotten to let Blackie out of the pasture before getting on. Jimmy inched his way up onto Blackie's neck and reached down to open the gate. Off he slid. He jumped up quickly and dusted his pants so Mama would not know that he had fallen. Then Jimmy led Blackie through the open gate. He climbed upon the gate again and back up onto Blackie's back. This time he had forgotten to latch the gate. The cow might wander out if the gate was not latched. Again, Jimmy inched his way almost to the horse's head and wrapped his arms around Blackie's neck and swung off. He latched the gate, and again he climbed onto the gate and back onto the horse.

Mabel went outside and pinned the note to his overalls and placed the sack of peppers into his hand.

Finally, Jimmy got to the store and traded the peppers for lard. "How are you going to get back on your horse?" asked a customer.

"Look out the window and you will see," answered Mr. Hilton, the store keeper. "Anytime that boy wants to ride, the horse goes to a gate or a wooden fence so the lad can climb back on."

"I'd love to have a horse like that for my boy."

"Yes, wouldn't we all," answered Mr. Hilton.

Jimmy gave the lard to Mama and she thanked God again for supplying what she needed. "I can make some fine bread when Alvin returns with the flour."

As Alvin and Cornelius were driving toward Mr. Hunter's farm to get the flour, Cornelius said, "I'm thankful you still have a car. These last few years have drained me of everything I owned."

"We lost almost everything except this car." Alvin said. "I wonder if our country is ever gonna come out of this recession?"

Slapping his hand on his knee, Cornelius stated, "I haven't had a steady job in four years now. My poor young'uns haven't decent clothes nor shoes. If things don't change, I'm afraid we won't be able to keep sending them to school."

"It must be really hard to keep five young'uns in decent clothes and shoes. I've only Jimmy in school. Mabel is really good about keeping his new pair of overalls clean, but sometimes she can't, and he has to wear his old overalls that are too short for him. Also, she makes him put on his old shoes or go barefoot at home to save his good shoes. Hopefully, I will be able to grow vegetables and sell them this summer and buy clothes for my family. Mabel really needs another dress."

After they picked up the flour, they went to Cornelius' house, divided the flour, and Alvin was soon home.

"Just look here," Alvin said with a big smile as he carried in the heavy sack of flour. "Here's our empty sack with flour in it again."

"And look what I have," Mabel held up the lard. "I traded our hot peppers for it."

"Capable in business, another virtue of a Proverbs 31 woman," he said. "You are the best. But isn't it amazing how God works things out for us to have whatever we need? It's just like we've often said, 'working together and trusting God we can conquer any problem.'"

Mabel made fluffy buttermilk biscuits and she served them with milk gravy for a late breakfast. They thanked God for providing the food. Then they ate. Oh, so yummy!

Questions for discussion:

1. For what did Alvin pray?
2. Why did Cornelius come to the farm?
3. How far did Cornelius walk?
4. How did God supply flour?
5. Did Jimmy help Mama?
6. How did Mabel get lard?
7. What kind of a woman is Mabel?

This 1926 Reo is owned by Craig Shaffer. It is similar to the one that Alvin had when he and Mabel married in 1929. God enabled him to keep it during the cruel years of the Great Depression and the Dust Bowl. In 1938 or 1939 he converted it into a pickup and used it for hauling coal which provided more income for his family.

5 Where is Roberta?

For he shall give his angels charge over thee, to keep thee in all thy ways. Psalm 91:11

"Me go with you?" Roberta begged as Alvin was putting on his hat to go plow in the potato field.

"Sure, come on," Alvin said, and taking Roberta by the hand, he led her to the barnyard. She waited patiently while he harnessed Ted, the horse, and hooked on the plow. Then he put her up on Ted's back. Blackie hobbled up as if he wanted to go work also, but Blackie was too old and stiff to work. Bob petted Blackie and he nuzzled her. Bob held onto Ted's mane to keep from falling as daddy led the horse toward the field. Blackie trotted along the fence, neighing as they went away.

"Always stay behind me so the horse doesn't step on you," Daddy told Roberta when he took her off Ted's back.

Alvin flipped over the plow, pushed the steel plow point into the ground and called, "Giddy-up" to Ted. Ted pulled forward. The plow sliced into the sod and rolled it upside down. Now the grass was under the dirt. On and on across the field they went, turning the sod upside down. This left a furrow (a long shallow ditch). Stepping along in the furrow, she followed her beloved daddy behind the plow across the field.

At the end of the field near the fence, Alvin turned Ted around. Again, he pushed the point of the plow into the ground and called, "Giddy-up." Ted pulled forward and the plow again sliced the hard earth and turned the sod over. Step by step Roberta followed him again as he plowed another furrow across the field. Back and forth they walked across the field.

By lunch time, Daddy had two wide portions of the potato field plowed. He unhooked the plow, placed Roberta on Ted again, and they walked back to the barnyard. Ted had worked hard all morning pulling the plow, so he was hungry and thirsty. When he saw the animal's watering tank be began trotting. She bounced up and down on his back. Alvin pitched Ted some hay and they walked into the house and found Mabel setting bowls of beans on the table beside a skillet of steaming cornbread. "Hmm, I'm hungry," said Alvin.

Alvin napped a while after eating, but Roberta did not sleep. She was afraid of missing the chance of returning to the field with her beloved daddy.

All afternoon she again trailed Alvin as he followed Ted and the plow back and forth, back and forth across the field. Alvin had to keep his eyes on the plow and keep it pushed down deep into the earth. If he didn't pay close attention, the plow would flip up out of the ground. He also had to keep his eyes on the end of the row to keep the rows straight.

In the late afternoon, he noticed that Roberta was not following him. "I am surprised that she knew her way back to the house," he said aloud. "She is a smart little girl and brave."

The sun was setting when Alvin ended a row, laid his plow over on its side and turned old Ted toward the house. It had been a good day. He had plowed a good portion of the field getting it ready to plant early red potatoes. He would have just enough time to see if the log under the sweet potato bed was still smoldering.

As he neared the house, he was happy to see Jimmy feeding and watering the chickens. He unharnessed Ted and gave him a scoop of grain and some hay. He would have to hurry and milk the cow. First, he went to check on the hot smoldering log, then he hurried into the house. As he was reaching for the milking pail just inside the door, Mabel asked, "Where is Roberta?"

Alvin whirled around and faced her. "She isn't here?"

"No, you took her this afternoon."

"She hasn't been following me for hours. I thought she had come back to the house.

"Oh!" Mabel explained. "How will we find her in the dark? She may have wandered off into the woods. Jimmy have you seen Roberta since you came home from school?"

"No, Mama."

"Have you, Lois?"

"No."

"How about you, Dink?"

"Me no see Bob."

"There is no telling where she might be," Alvin said. "I'll fill the lantern and go searching. I can milk the cow later using lantern light. You all pray that I will find her. Are you sure she isn't here? Surely she is around here somewhere. Maybe she is asleep."

"She could be, she didn't take a nap when you did," Mabel said in a desperate tone.

Mr. Broady was gone, so Alvin looked in his room. "She's not in there." He knelt down and looked under his and Mabel's bed, raised up and said. "Remember that time Cornelius' boy, Tom, got lost and we were hunting all over the neighborhood and Grandma found him asleep under his bed?"

"Yes, I remember," Mabel answered. "I hope our search turns out like that. But hurry, she may have awakened in the dark and is somewhere frightened and crying."

"Okay, but I want to look around here first."

"Maybe she is in the smokehouse. The girls sometimes play in there," Mabel suggested.

"Come on, Jimmy," Alvin said, "you can look in one direction while I look in the other."

Together they walked all around the outside of the house. Then they searched inside and outside of the shed, the chicken house, and the smokehouse. They hunted through the barn, hoping to find Roberta asleep somewhere on a pile of hay. Mabel was standing in the doorway watching as Alvin carried the lantern from place to place. Lois stood close beside her.

"I'm headed for the field. Pray I'll find her," Alvin called back to Mabel.

Mabel went inside and knelt on the floor and prayed, then Lois and Dink prayed.

Alvin prayed as he walked, "Please, God, guide me to Roberta. You know exactly where she is." He held his lantern high over his head so it would shine out over a larger portion of the field. He saw nothing. He walked along the side of the plowed field. Nothing. They walked around the edges of the woods looking for her asleep under a tree. Nothing.

He thought surely she would not be in center of the field. However, as if guided by God's spirit, he walked out into the part he had plowed that day. Down one row then another he walked, looking all around. Suddenly he came upon her, hidden from sight, lying asleep in the bottom of a furrow. He touched her and said, "Wake up, Bob, it's time to go home. Here, Jimmy, take the lantern." Jimmy took the lantern and Daddy lifted Bob up into his arms. Her sleepy head fell heavily upon his shoulder. It felt so good to have his precious little Roberta snuggled in the crook of his neck. "Thank you, Jesus. Thank you for taking care of my little shadow. You are so good."

Mabel was again standing in the door when he neared the house. Jimmy held the lantern high so Mabel could see Bob's sleepy head on Daddy's shoulder. Mabel stretched her arms toward heaven and said, "Oh thank you, God, thank you for hearing our cries."

Questions for discussion:

1. Who did Bob love to follow?
2. Where did Alvin believe Bob had gone?
3. Why did they not look for Bob sooner?
4. How did Alvin find Bob?
5. Who was watching over Bob?
6. Who will watch over us if we should get lost?

6 A Summer with Grandma and Grandpa

Foolishness is bound in the heart of a child; but the rod of correction will drive it far from him.
Proverbs 22:15

The spring sunshine warmed the Broady Farm east of Del City, Oklahoma. Red Fire-bush and golden Scotch Broom bloomed near the front door. Sand plums along the fence rows and blackberries along the creek banks were covered with white blossoms. Grapes, red crabapple and other wild fruit were also budding.

To Alvin and Mabel, it was like paradise. The cow had given birth to a calf and was now giving them more milk than they needed. There was enough to share with Cornelius' family and Grandma and Grandpa Hightower whenever they could come and get it. When they did not come for the milk, Mabel made cottage cheese. First, she heated the milk; then after the milk clabbered, she poured off the whey and poured the curds into a small cloth sack. She hung the sack on her clothesline until all the whey dripped out, leaving a ball of firm curds. This she crumbled into a bowl, sprinkled on a little salt, and added to it some thick cream. It made delicious cottage cheese.

Early spring rains caused the wild fruit crop to look so promising that Grandpa and Grandma Hightower wanted to help Mabel pick and preserve this fruit that would soon be ripening. There was no money for gasoline to drive the seven miles back and forth each day from their home, so they moved in with Alvin's family on the Broady farm.

As soon as the fruit began ripening, Mabel, Grandma, Grandpa and the girls went to the woods every few days. They picked the fruit as it ripened: white mulberries, sand plums, dewberries, and later on blackberries. In the afternoons they washed and boiled the fruit with sugar to make jam.

Grandpa was tall and thin. He had a long white beard and handlebar mustache. Dink thought he was skinny because the hair over his mouth kept him from eating. When he sat down to eat, Dink sat close to him so she could see if he ate. She was surprised when he put the spoon into his mouth. "Howd you know where your mouth is?" she asked.

"I know where it is just like you know where your mouth is," he answered.

"But me no can find me mouf if me hairs on it," she answered. Everyone laughed.

Alvin had dug up a small patch of ground on the south side of the big barn and planted spinach, radishes, green onions and early potatoes, which were now ready to eat. His early sweet potato plants would soon be bringing a good price at the Farmers Market. Also, his own crop of early potatoes was growing rapidly in the warm bed he had made on the east side of the barn. Alvin went about his days whistling. He was full of hope for a successful year. He had already planted another large field of red potatoes which he planned to sell.

One morning when Mama was washing clothes and Grandma, Lois and Grandpa had gone again into the woods looking for fruit and greens, Bob saw Dink climbing up the windmill. "Don't climb on that," Bob shouted to her. Dink kept on climbing. Bob tried again to stop her; but Dink began climbing faster, so Bob ran to the house calling, "Mama, Mama, Dink is climbing up the windmill." Mama dropped the overalls she was scrubbing and ran around the corner of the house. By then Dink was far up on the tall windmill and yelling for the world to look at her. Mabel grew pale. It was a windy day and the blades at the top of the windmill were turning fast. "Oh, Lord," Mabel cried, "spare my child from being mangled by those sharp speeding blades." Mabel could not climb the windmill and get Dink down.

"No afraid, Mommy. I be right."

"Hold on tight, and don't go any higher," Mabel ordered.

Alvin was away working in the back field. Mr. Broady had gone to town. Where was Grandpa?

"Run to the woods and see if you can find Grandpa. He could get here before Daddy," Mabel shouted to Bob.

Bob ran across the barnyard toward the wooded area, yelling, "Grandpa, Grandpa, come quick, Dink's about to kill herself."

Grandpa heard Bob calling and came running. He looked up at the towering windmill with a three-year-old hanging near the top. "It seems that child was born to cause a ruckus," he said. "She's always doing something ridiculously dangerous. How can I reach her? I'm too old to climb this windmill."

"Someone's got to save her. Those blades will knock her to the ground," pleaded Mabel.

"I don't think I can, but I will try," he said, and started climbing.

When Dink saw him, she giggled and started climbing higher. "Stop! Stop!" Mabel demanded. "Oh, Lord help us," she begged.

Grandpa went cautiously on and on, higher and higher. To Dink it was a funny game.

By now, Grandma and Lois were there, looking up at the dangerous blades whirling just above Dink's head. Grandma began praying with Mabel. Lois joined in.

Grandpa was higher, getting nearer to Dink. Dink giggled and started climbing again. "Stop!" Grandpa ordered. Dink stopped and looked down at him. Then turned as if to climb again. Mabel covered her eyes. "Stop!" Grandpa demanded again. All the while, Grandpa was slowly climbing higher. Dink turned her face upward—Grandpa grabbed her foot.

Grandpa was out of breath. His heart was weak, and he hadn't climbed a windmill in years. He rested for a moment, then brought her down.

"All right little Miss Smarty Pants," Mabel scolded, "come here." She took Dink into their bedroom. She closed the door and followed the instructions of Proverbs 13:24. *He that spares the rod hates his son: but he that loves his son chastens him be times.* Dink cried herself to sleep. Never again did she climb the windmill, but that did not stop her from climbing in the barn, on the smokehouse, the shed and trees. In despair, Mabel exclaimed again, and again, "I wonder if this child will live to be grown?"

Week after week Alvin watched the sky for signs of rain as he continued clearing brush, plowing and harrowing the fields. He wanted to plant corn, beans, tomatoes, melons and cucumbers. Each evening during worship the family prayed for rain.

Day after day the ground became dryer and dryer. The fierce wind picked up the loose, dry topsoil and blew it up into his face then carried it far away. Day by day his hopes faded until one evening he came in and threw his hat on the floor. Mabel whirled around, for Alvin never acted like that. "This drought is destroying my hopes and dreams of this farm being our lifesaver. There isn't enough moisture to keep anything alive. The little potato plants all over the field are bowing down their little heads begging for a drink. The cornfields are ready to plant, but no rain. If God doesn't send rain, there will be no crops; and come winter, we will be in the same condition we were last winter," he said.

"Surely God will send rain soon," Mabel answered. "We can be thankful for the little rain that helped the spring garden and the early potatoes to grow. We are also grateful that the well hasn't gone dry."

"Yes, I am thankful for that. And I'm glad Grandma is keeping the early potatoes alive by watering them from a bucket. But they are being eaten up by potato bugs. We need to get the children out there today and pick off the bugs."

"Okay. I'll do that today," replied Mabel.

"Grandpa is itching to help me plant; but we can't plant until we have some moisture, although I have seeds and the ground is ready!"

"I'm so sorry," Mabel said. "But Alvin, always remember: 'working together and trusting in God we have conquered our other problems.' Also remember we will have jam for our bread this winter. We made mulberry and blackberry jelly today, and the wild grapes and currents are ripening. I suppose their roots are long and they are finding moisture deep down in the earth."

"Must be," Alvin answered, "for there is none on top."

That afternoon Mabel put a little kerosene into three cans and gave one each to Jimmy, Lois and Bob. She took them into the potato patch and showed them how to pick off the potato bugs and drop the bugs into the cans.

After picking potato bugs, the children were free to explore the woods and the farm. Grandpa taught them many things about the different plants and insects they found. Sitting outside in the cool of the evening, they listened to Grandpa's and Grandma's stories of life long ago. During worship, they sang some of Grandma's and Alvin's new songs.

"Jesus Set Me Free"

Sinner was I without my Lord
I did not know His Holy Word.
I lived for self, the world and sin
That changed when Jesus came in.

Chorus
Till Jesus set me free
There was no victory
But Jesus is my Jubilee
For He has set me free.

Happy am I to know my Lord
To read His Precious Holy Word.
I love to sing, rejoice and pray
While walking in His gracious way.

Longing am I to be at home
With my Savior around His throne.
I know my name is written there
My hope's in Him, glories to share.
By Lou Hightower

Sometimes they sang Alvin's "Sow the Seed" or another song he had written.

Sow the seed in every field
Time will bring the golden yield.
Sow the seed, sow the seed.
See the fields so great and white
And the laborers so few.

Sow the precious heavenly seed.

Hear the Master calls for thee
Time is swiftly passing by
Sow the seed, sow the seed.
See the evening sun hangs low
And the sowing time soon o'er
Sow the precious heavenly seed.

Soon the sowing time will end
Many souls will die in sin.
Sow the seed, sow the seed.
Then the lost will mourn and sigh,
To that awful darkness fly.
Sow the precious heavenly seed.

Oh, my brother heed the call,
See the Savior needs us all,
Sow the seed, sow the seed.
Come ye sowers one and all
For the sowing must be done.
Sow the precious heavenly seed.

Although they sang and played with Grandma and Grandpa on the farm, the drought never left their minds. Every day they prayed for rain.

What a sad day when Grandma and Grandpa packed up their things to leave. Dink was crying. Grandpa was saying good-bye to Roberta by *ruffing her up* with his stickery whiskers. Lois was clinging to Grandma. "Please don't go," Lois begged. "We don't want you to leave."

"Frosty nights will eventually be here, and you will want to sleep in your warm bed. Also, the persimmons will be sweet and ready to pick. Be sure to bring me some ripe persimmons when you come," Grandma said. She kissed each one, then said to Mabel, "It has been wonderful being here, but we must go now. Alvin and Jimmy are in the car waiting for us."

"Tell Mr. Broady good-bye for us," Grandpa said.

Each one followed Grandma and Grandpa outside and waved until the car disappeared when Alvin turned out of the lane onto the highway.

After Grandma and Grandpa had gone, the rain they had prayed for so long finally came. It was a gentle rain. Every drop moistened the dry parched soil.

Questions for discussion:

1. For what were Mabel and Alvin thankful?
2. Why did Grandma and Grandpa come to the farm?
3. Did Mabel obey God's Word?
4. What will the 'rod of correction' do for a child?
5. What did they do in the evenings?
6. How did they solve their problems?
7. Did God send rain?

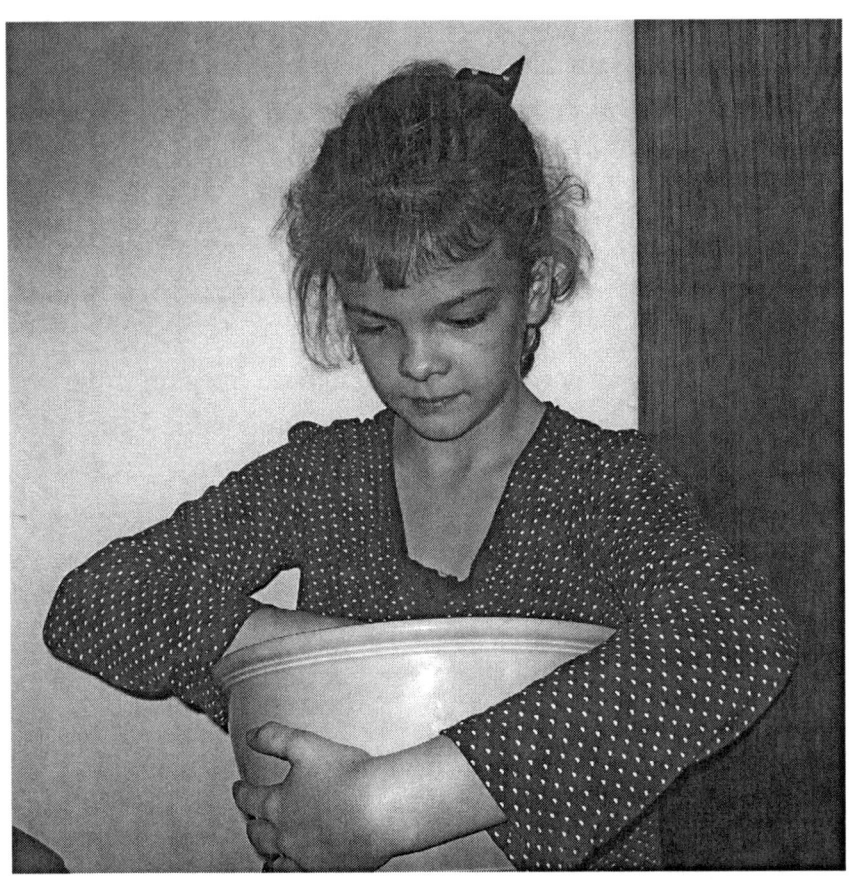

Grandma would pour a five-pound bag of flour into this bowl. Each morning she added a little lard, baking powder, salt, and milk. Then, she would form a few biscuits with the top layer of flour, and leave the remaining amount of flour dry. She did this until the bowl was empty, and then she would fill the bowl again.

7 Buried Alive!

For thou, Lord, art good, and ready to forgive; and plenteous in mercy unto all them that call upon thee.
Psalms 86:5

Grandma and Grandpa were back in their home in south Oklahoma City. Grandma had worked all day getting her house clean after being away at the farm all summer. It was late, but she was just preparing supper when a man knocked at the door. He was out of breath from running. "Oh, Miss—I've come—with bad news," he said between gasps of breath. "Some hooded men caught Cornelius, drug him into a car and have taken him away."

"Oh, Lord have mercy on my boy," Grandma Lou groaned. "They must be of the Ku Klux Klan. I've been hearing they are doing terrible things. And Cornelius has been hanging around with some of 'em. Say do you know someone who has a car and can go tell Alvin? He will know just what we should do."

"Sure, Miss, I can get a car. Where shall I go to find Alvin?"

"He lives on the Broady farm, seven miles east of town. You take 29th Street all the way till you get to a little store away out of town, then turn right into the lane in front of the store. That is where the Broady farm is."

A Faithful Father

"Yes. I'll fetch him for you."

The Ku Klux Klan had been active in Oklahoma for many years. At one time, it boasted 95,000 members in Oklahoma and 190,000 in Texas. "Its primary message in 1920 was that it stood for law and order, traditional morality and most importantly, *'100 percent Americanism.'* The Klan's *100 percent Americanism* included only white Americans, and that allowed them to target blacks, Jews, radicals, immigrants from any country–even Mexicans–and especially Catholics."

The Ku Klux Klan members on duty dressed in white robes, pointed hats and masks that completely covered their heads. Under this protective garb, the members hid their clubs, knives, ropes and their identity. They were involved in widespread public whippings, tar feathering, lynching, and brutal homicides. At one time, they burned 35 square blocks of homes in Greenwood, a section of Tulsa where Blacks lived. Oklahoma City had escaped such horrendous action, but many individuals had been whipped, tarred, burned, raped, and slaughtered in various ways.

(www.okhistory.org)

Alvin's family and his parents had no prejudices against any race. They attended church and worked and played together with Blacks. They labored peacefully side by side with Jews, Mexicans and German immigrants. They were also censured as being radicals because of their religious beliefs in divine healing. They were a prime target for the Ku Klux Klan; however, because they attended to their own business and trusted God, so far He had protected them. Cornelius had strayed away from his Christian training and was chumming around with men who knew a lot about the Klan's activities.

When Alvin arrived at Grandma's house, quite a number of neighbors had already gathered outside. Grandma was keeping

Cornelius' children inside her house. "They said they were going to bury him alive," a neighbor shouted to Alvin as he was getting out of his car.

"And they will," another assured.

"'Em Ku Klux Klan folks are a heartless bunch," another man said. "We've gotta get Cornelius away from 'em or they's likely to kill him."

"Alvin, we will help you. Let's go find 'em!"

"Oh, no don't do that. They will come and burn youns houses down too. You'd best not mess with them folks," another answered. The group kept shouting first one suggestion then another. Some were threatening to burn the houses of some Klan members that they knew. Others were boasting about their strength.

Alvin listened for a few minutes and then cleared his throat. "I tell you what, men," Alvin spoke in his usual soft voice. They all stopped talking and listened. "God is bigger than the Ku Klux Klan. He is still in control. We will humble ourselves before God and ask for His mercy. If God doesn't help us, Cornelius is a goner. Let's all just bow our heads and pray." The men took off their hats and bowed their heads. Many held their hats over their heart. Alvin bowed on one knee and began praying. "Our dear heavenly Father, we humble ourselves before You and beg your mighty help. Cornelius has a family that needs him. His motherless children really need him, for he has to be both their mother and their daddy, and he has to work to provide for these orphans. Now you know that Cornelius has been dabbling in things that he ought not; but, Jesus, have mercy on him for his children's sake. Put your big hand over him, and do whatever you need to do to defeat the plans of the men who wish to harm Cornelius. In Jesus' name we humbly ask this. Amen."

"Now I need a couple of men to disguise yourselves so you won't be recognized to go out to find where they have taken him. But don't let anyone know who you are or you will be in big trouble with the

Klan. Just a couple of light-footed men who will work together and who know how to walk in the woods without making noise." Some men volunteered. "May God bless you and do be careful!"

Alvin dismissed the other men and went into the house to calm Grandma, who was crying uncontrollably. He put his arms around her and said, "Remember, Mom, God is in control. He can stop the Klan from doing their dirty work."

Grandma looked up at Alvin, her face stained with tears. "But what will we do without Cornelius? I'm trying to take their mother's place, but I can't provide for them. Who's going to pay for their food and clothes? Ezra and Aubrey are not here to help. You can hardly supply for your own. Grandpa isn't able to work a job if there was a job to be had. I thought things couldn't get worse, but they have."

"Mom, get control of yourself. Where is your faith? Don't throw it away. Now is when you need it."

"Yes, I know, I know. But why has this happened?"

"Don't ask why. Just pray for God's mercy," Alvin said, as he knelt down and began praying out loud. Grandma and Grandpa joined him. They prayed and they waited for news, Grandma crying all the while. They prayed again and waited.

"You suppose they took Cornelius thinking your Aunt Mary would pay a ransom to get him released? A lot of people know she has money, because she has been buying up properties."

"I don't think so, Mom. But don't worry about it. God has promised to help his children and we are his children."

"Both you boys have lost everything you owned. Then Montella *taken* sick and stayed six weeks in the hospital. Now the children are motherless. What will we do if they are orphans of both mom and dad? And who is going to pay Montella's hospital and funeral bills? As I said, I didn't think things could get worse but they have." Grandma covered her face and began sobbing again.

Alvin felt bewildered as to how to comfort her. Mabel faced everything with faith and courage. "Please, Mom, please, trust me, trust God; everything is possible if we trust in God." He held her tight in his arms until she stopped sobbing. Then they prayed again. Far into the night they were still praying and waiting. In the dark hours of the new day, they dozed off to sleep.

As the day was dawning, a car stopped in front of Grandma's house and Cornelius got out. He staggered toward the house while two of the neighbor men were helping him walk. Grandma heard the noise and met him at the door. "Oh, son, thank God you are alive," she said as she hugged him. "We prayed all night for God to have mercy on you."

"That's what saved me," he admitted.

"Tell us what happened," Grandpa said.

"Okay," Cornelius said, "let me get *set* down and drink some water." Grandma scurried away to the water bucket and brought back a dipper full of water. Then she gave a dipper full of water to each of the other men. By this time, his older children had awakened and gathered in. They sat on the floor in front of him.

"Well, it was this way. They hauled me into the woods to a newly dug grave. I fought with all my might, but there isn't much one feller can do against four others. The next thing I knew, here comes two more fellas carrying a big wooden box. Between the six of 'em they crammed me into the box and me a *fight'n* as hard as I could. Then they nailed on the lid. I was so cramped I could not move in any way. My breath came short. I thought sure I was dying, so I began begging for God's mercy. Then I felt myself sliding down into the big hole. After the box hit the bottom, I could hear the dirt falling on it as they were shoveling it in.

"That was the most horrendous feeling! In my mind, I saw my orphan children standing around my grave weeping, fear on their faces. I saw you, Mom, and you, Dad, grieving your hearts out.

While I was listening to the dirt fall on the box, I was struggling to breathe, to stay alive. Oh, it was all so horrible. I want to forget it all. To be buried alive is like hell," he wailed and covered his face as if to shut out something he was seeing.

Alvin walked over and put his hand on Cornelius' shoulder. "Let's have prayer, brother, and thank God for bringing you back alive." Then he knelt on one knee and began praying. Cornelius slid off his chair onto his knees and buried his face in the chair cushion. Then Grandpa, Grandma, the other men and the children bowed on their knees while Alvin was praying.

After praying, Pete, his oldest son, said, "We're so glad you got away from those guys. Daddy, how'd you get loose?"

"Children, I thought you had lost your daddy as well as your mother. I was fighting to breathe to stay alive for you all, but I thought I was a goner. All this time, I was praying for God to help me. After a while, I felt a quaking. A bit later, I felt something heavy on my casket. I guess it was Joe when he jumped in to throw out the dirt. I felt like hollering, but feared if it was the Klan, I wanted 'em to think I was already dead. But thank God it was these old boys right here, and he slapped each one on their knee. These guys saved me alive. They dug the dirt off the casket, ripped it open and helped me out."

Questions for discussion:

1. What had happened to Cornelius?
2. Who did Grandma call to help?
3. What was Alvin's advice?
4. Who could control the Ku Klux Klan?
5. What did the family and friends do at Grandma's house?
6. What did the hooded men do to Cornelius?
7. Who kept Cornelius alive?

8 Hit by a Speeding Car

Children, obey your parents in the Lord: for this is right. Ephesians 6:1

"Can we sing as soon as the dishes are finished?" Lois asked, when she and Mabel were washing supper dishes.

"Yes, Lord willing we will sing again every night after supper as soon as the crops are all gathered," Mabel answered.

Alvin interrupted, "Yes we will. It's been so wonderful having rain this summer; but of course, I had to work very much and not had much time for family worship. But things will be back to normal in a few more weeks. Then we can sing, read the Bible and pray every evening."

"And have a story?" Bob questioned.

"Yes, we will read the Bible and have a story, too," he promised.

"We are going to have a story," Roberta told Dink. "We like stories don't we?" Dink clapped her hands.

"What shall we sing first?" Mabel asked.

"Let's sing, 'Come to me,' " Lois suggested.

"Is this the one you want?" Mabel asked, and began singing, "I am so glad that the Savior has said, 'Come unto me, come unto me.'"

Lois shook her head, "Yes."

As soon as the dishes were put away, they sat down and began singing, "What the Savior Hath Said," written by B.E. Warren.

> "I am so glad that the Savior has said,
> 'Come unto me, come unto me.'
> When he bestowed on each little one's head.
> Blessings so rich and free.
>
> Chorus
> Come to the Savior dear children today.
> Come, let us walk in the heavenly way;
> Sweet is the promise to those who obey;
> Come, there is room for all.

When they finished singing it, Jimmy asked to sing, "I'm Going On," so they sang:

> "I mean to go right on until the crown is won;
> I mean to fight the fight of faith 'Til life on earth is done.
> I'll never more turn back! Defeat I shall not know.
> For God will give me victory as onward I shall go."
> C.W. Naylor

"'Defeat I shall not know. For God will give me victory' should be another motto for us," Alvin said. "God gives victory to those who are determined to trust in him. I'll tell you the story of David. He had many problems, but God gave him victory over each one." While Daddy was telling the story, Bob climbed up on the bed and curled up like a kitten on the thick straw mattress. Before Daddy finished the story, she had fallen asleep.

After all the children were asleep, Alvin said, "Makes me feel good that the children like family worship. Before we were married, I promised God if he gave me children that I would teach them God's Word. Children need spiritual food every day, just as they need food for their bodies each day. I want our children to go to sleep with songs of Zion ringing in their ears and God's Word freshly planted in their hearts."

"That is also my desire," Mabel replied. "When I was young, I loved God's Word. Although at the time, I did not understand my soul's need for spiritual food; I just knew that reading the Bible comforted me, and it also gave me courage to do what I thought I should do. Our children have their difficulties, and they need comfort and courage from God's Word. Well, that is, all except for Charlotte. She has more courage (or foolishness, which ever it is) than she needs. I am so thankful to be out here in the country away from streets and the railroad. Now I'm not afraid she will get hit by a car or a train. I think all the children are safer here."

"Yes, this is a very safe place to live."

The following morning, Alvin drove into the city because he had a job to finish. In the afternoon while Charlotte was asleep, Mabel said to Jimmy, "I am going to hurry to the little store. You stay here and take care of your sisters. If Dink wakes up, be sure to latch the door to keep her safe in the house. I don't want her climbing the smokehouse or the windmill or wandering off down to the highway and get hit by a car. Stay right here until I come back."

"Yes, ma'am," Jimmy answered.

Mabel took off her apron and started toward the store. She looked back several times as she walked down the lane to be sure that none of the children were following her. At the highway, she looked back again and then crossed the highway and went into the store.

Jimmy waited until Mama was out of sight, and then, he too, started down the lane. "Look, Jimmy is leaving us and Mama told him to stay right here," Lois told Roberta.

"He's going to get into trouble," Bob answered. "But I'm afraid to stay here without him."

"Me, too. Let's go with him," Lois said. Then, taking Bob by the hand, they started down the lane.

Each time Mabel went to the store, she looked at the pretty sacks of flour. It took two flour sacks to make a small dress and four to make one for herself. She needed a new dress. Rain was falling regularly, so Alvin was doing well selling vegetables. She had money in her purse to buy two sacks. How badly she wanted to find two identical to the ones she already had. While Mabel was focusing on the patterns on the flour sacks, she heard a woman shout, "A car hit that little boy!"

I'm thankful my children were safe at home, Mabel thought.

Then she heard the store keeper say, "That boy belongs to the Hightower family that lives on the Broady farm."

"What? Is that my boy?" Mabel exclaimed, as she hurried out of the store. She threw herself to her knees beside Jimmy's still body and prayed, "Lord, please help, spare Jimmy. He's our only son."

Jimmy opened his eyes, and mumbled, "I'm alright."

By now everyone in the store had gathered around. The driver was saying, "I'm sorry madam, but the child ran right out in front of me. I tried to dodge him. Shall I carry him to the hospital?"

"No, just take us home, please. We live at the end of that lane." She pointed to the driveway, then added, "I told him to stay at home. I am surprised that he disobeyed."

The driver lifted Jimmy carefully into the back seat of his car. Mabel climbed in beside him. When they got to the house, Alvin had just arrived. "What happened?" he asked, when he saw Mabel holding Jimmy in the stranger's car.

"Jimmy disobeyed and followed me to the store."

The stranger jumped out and hurried around the car and said to Alvin, "I'm sorry, sir, but he ran right in front of me. I couldn't avoid him. I tried really hard. Is there anything I can do?"

"Some things we just can't help," Alvin said. "Hopefully, he isn't seriously hurt. Thanks for bringing him and Mabel to the house. We will see that he gets good care."

Bob and Lois came running out of the house. When Bob saw Jimmy lying in the car, she asked, "Is he dead?"

Alvin put his arms around Roberta, looked into her eyes and said, "No, Bob, your brother will be alright. God will help him."

"We saw the car hit him, so we ran inside and hid," Lois told Mama. "We didn't want you to know that we were following you, too."

Mabel gasped. Jimmy opened his eyes and smiled at Lois.

"Is there anything I can do?" asked the stranger again.

"No," Alvin said. Then he carried Jimmy gently to the bed. He examined Jimmy by moving his arms and legs and feeling all over his body for broken bones. "There are no broken bones," he said.

After the man who hit Jimmy left, Mabel took off Jimmy's pants and shirt. She cleaned the seventeen cuts and scrapes.

"We will need to watch him closely. Other problems may show up later," Alvin said.

"Yes, I will watch him carefully. I was really surprised that he disobeyed and followed me. I thought my children were safe. He is usually an obedient boy, but I see even good children can be tempted. This will probably be a lesson that he will never forget. We must also trust God with this problem and work together. You

A Faithful Father

girls will need to help nurse Jimmy and do the chores that he was doing until he is well," Mama said.

"We will Mommy," the girls chimed in.

Questions for discussion:

1. What did the family do each evening?
2. What did they do during family worship?
3. What did Bob like best?
4. What did Mabel tell Jimmy to do?
5. What were Lois and Bob doing?
6. What happened to Jimmy? Why?

9 Bringing in the Hay

While the earth remains, seedtime and harvest, and cold and heat, and summer and winter, and day and night shall not cease. Genesis 8:22

Alvin and Jimmy walked across the hayfield. "It's a good time to harvest," Alvin said. "No sign of rain and the grass is in perfect condition."

Back in the barnyard, he and Jimmy oiled the mower and checked the ropes that would lift the big heavy hay fork loaded with hay into the barn. "Looks like I need to replace this rope. Every rope must be strong. Jimmy, run to the store and get me 50 feet of rope this size." He cut off a piece of the old tattered rope and handed it to Jimmy.

The following morning as the day was dawning, Alvin was hooking the team, Ted and Ginger, to the mowing machine. To protect himself from the burning August sun, Alvin wore overalls, a shirt, denim jacket and straw hat with a heavy rag under the hat that hung down over his neck. Haying weather was always hot. It needed to be hot so the hay could dry quickly.

Alvin started cutting close to the fences. He cut the hay so that it fell inside the field. Every blade would be needed to feed the animals during the cold winter. When he had cut one strip all around the field, he turned the horse around and went the opposite direction around the field so the hay would fall on what he had just cut and away from the uncut hay. Around and around the field the horses pulled the clattering mowing machine, always cutting from the outside toward the center so the grass fell on hay that had already been cut.

The frightened rabbits, snakes, and other wild creatures that lived in the field scurried into the center to hide in the tall uncut grass. When the tall grass in the center became only a narrow strip, the many wild creatures came popping out and dashing across the mown field toward the thick fence rows. "Wish I could shoot 'em rabbits and have 'em for supper," Alvin mumbled. "And there sure is a bunch of snakes scootin' away. I hope an old rattler don't hide under the hay and bite someone when they pick up the shock."

Mid-morning Jimmy came with hot biscuits and salt pork sandwiches and a quart jar of water for Alvin. While Alvin ate, Jimmy rubbed Ted and Ginger with a wet rag to cool them. Jimmy wanted to ride on the mowing machine, but Alvin knew it was too dangerous. If Jimmy accidentally fell, the horses might get spooked and go racing away wildly and cause much damage.

Ted and Ginger were wet with sweat around noon when Alvin turned them toward the watering trough. He, too, felt like he could drink a gallon of cool water. It had been a good morning. Alvin had finished mowing the smallest field. He would finish another small patch in the afternoon. He could then mow the larger field while the hay in the smaller fields was drying. Alvin wanted the hay well dried. Freshly cut hay, if packed in the barn before drying, could through spontaneous combustion, burst into flames and burn the barn down. He sure didn't want that to happen.

When the hay was dried, Grandpa, Uncle Cornelius and his older boys, Pete and Bill, came to help put the hay in the barn. Grandma came to help Mabel cook for the hungry workers.

While Alvin was hooking Ted and Ginger to the *dump rake*, Cornelius said, "My boys and I can pile it into shocks."

"And Jimmy and I can also do some," Grandpa added.

They followed Alvin to the field, and while he raked the hay into windrows, they were making cone shaped hay shocks. "These hay shocks look like little tents," Jimmy remarked.

"They are kind of like tents because they protect the dry hay," Grandpa answered. "There is always fear that rain will ruin the hay after it is cut before it is taken into the barn. Having it in shocks is protecting it from heavy dew and light rain. Only a heavy rain can ruin the hay in a shock."

For three days they raked and made hay shocks. Mabel and Grandma cooked. Lois and Roberta carried cool water to the field for the thirsty workers.

Then came the big day! The day that Roberta loved. The neighbors came bringing their teams of horses hooked to hay wagons. Alvin already had his team hitched up to his wagon. Grandpa would drive Alvin's team, for he was unable to pitch the hay high into the wagon. Each man, with a long handled pitchfork in his hand, climbed onto the wagons. Then Pete, Jimmy and Bill got on.

"Can't I go?" Bob pleaded as Pete was helping her up.

"Not this time," Alvin answered, and lifted her down.

"Me too, wanta go," Dink wailed.

Alvin shook his head, "No."

Grandpa pulled the hay wagon into the field alongside a hay shock. The men jumped off and lined up two on each side of a hay shock. Standing on opposite sides of the hay shock, they placed their pitchforks into the hay shock and raised the entire shock onto the wagon with an overhead sweeping motion. The first shock was on the wagon. Grandpa moved the wagon to the next hay shock, and the two men beside that hay shock threw another shock of hay onto the wagon. The horses pulled the wagon to the next one. On and on the wagon moved across the field, as one by one the shocks were thrown upon the wagon. Jimmy, Bill and Pete trampled the fluffy hay down, making room for more and more hay. Sometimes a rattlesnake or a large blacksnake hiding in the hay shock would be slung onto the wagon along with the hay. Thankfully, that had not happened today.

When the wagon could hold no more hay, the boys climbed off his wagon and onto another. Grandpa drove the horses to the barn and another empty wagon took his place. It began moving from shock to shock as the men threw the hay over their heads and onto the flat wagon. The boys continued trampling hay.

Grandpa parked the wagon full of hay at one end of the barn under the big hay fork. The door at the roof level of the barn was built there to allow entry of the forks full of hay. The hay fork resembled a giant double fishhook tied to a heavy rope. The rope ran through a pulley at the roof level. The rope extended to the far end of the barn. A neighbor's team of horses was hitched to the end of this rope. When the hay fork was locked into a large load of hay, the horses would pull on the rope to raise the forkful of hay to the top of the barn. When it reached the top of the barn, the hay fork traveled the whole length of the barn on a trolley rail. That enabled the hay to be deposited anyplace in the barn. A trip rope was pulled to release the forkful of hay in the desired location. When the fork had deposited the hay, a man pulled the empty fork back over the hay wagon. The weight of the heavy fork caused it to go deep into the soft hay. When the fork was clamped tight, the team would again pull the forkful of hay up to the top of the barn and across the barn to the desired spot. The man below pulled the trip rope and another fork of hay was stored for the winter.

Lois, Roberta and Dink were standing by the smokehouse watching. Roberta said to Dink, "That fork lifts as much hay as the hand of God could lift."

"Is God that big?" Dink questioned.

"Oh, yes, He's bigger! He could hold all the hay in the barn in his hand."

"I didn't know God was that big."

After two fork loads of hay, the wagon was empty, so Grandpa went back to the field for more hay. Another wagonload of hay was on its way to the barn to be emptied just as Grandpa's was emptied.

All day one wagon after another came to the barn and the big hay fork carried the hay into the barn. The last load of hay was deposited into the barn loft just before dark.

The men washed their hands and faces at the pump above the animals' drinking trough beside the windmill. They sat down at a table Mabel had set under the tree and ate Grandma's famous chicken and dumplings, cornbread and wild blackberry pie that Mabel had made from blackberries she and the girls had picked.

For worship that night, Alvin read only one verse: Proverbs 6:6. *Go to the ant, thou sluggard; consider her ways, and be wise: Which having no guide, overseer, or ruler, provides her meat in the summer, and gathers her food in the harvest.* "Are we like ants?" Bob asked.

"With the neighbors here, and everyone working, we did look like ants today," Jimmy added.

"Yes, we are good workers, in this way we are like ants. Let's pray and thank God we will have hay for the animals this winter."

A Faithful Father

Questions for discussion:

1. Did God promise harvest until the end of the world? (verse)
2. How did Alvin protect himself from the sun?
3. Who came to help with the haying?
4. How did the girls help?
5. Of what did the hay fork remind Bob?
6. Did everyone work?
7. In what ways should we be like ants?

10 God's a Good Mechanic

If any of you lack wisdom, let him ask of God, that giveth to all men liberally, and upbraideth not; and it shall be given him. James 1:5

"Say Mabel, I have a lot of sweet potatoes I need to take to Pauls Valley today to be dried. Want to ride along with me?" Alvin asked, as he sat down at the breakfast table.

Jimmy, Lois and Bob were already sitting at the table. Dink was in her chair. Mabel set a plate of hot biscuits on the table, sat down and answered. "I am surprised that you have so many sweet potatoes left to dry after selling so many."

"We have had a bumper crop so much different from last year," Alvin said. "Think you want to go along with me?"

"I haven't been out for a while. It would probably do me good to get out. But we will have to be home before Lois and Jim get home from school. Mr. Broady said he's not coming back for a few days."

After Alvin had thanked God for the food, he said, "I think we can be home by 1:00 or 1:30. We will only need to unload the sweet potatoes and come right back." Then, turning to eight-year-old Jimmy, he said, "In case something unusual happens and we are delayed, you be sure the horses, the cows, the chickens, and the pig have water to drink. Just pump water into the watering trough for the horses and the cow. You will have to carry a bucket of water for the pig. It will be hard but I know you can do it. You are a big boy now. The chickens need only a half bucket of water."

"Yes, sir," Jimmy answered with his mouth full of fried potatoes.

"And another thing, Jimmy," Daddy continued, "none of this running to the neighbors to play. You are to take care of your little sister, Lois. She will be afraid if you are not with her all the time. Do you understand me?"

"Yes, sir," Jimmy answered again.

"I'll be expecting you to be right here when we get home. I hope we will be here before you, but if we are not, remember that I said, 'stay at home.'"

"Okay," Jim said, as he wiped up the last bit of his gravy with a biscuit.

Mabel made sandwiches of biscuits with blackberry jam and placed them into the lunch bucket for Lois and Jim to take to school. She gave them each a big squeeze and kissed them saying, "Good bye, and obey your teacher."

Alvin loaded the sweet potatoes into the car then drove close to the house to pick up his family. Roberta and Dink climbed into the back seat, then he opened the door for Mabel.

"Pauls Valley is about 60 miles," Daddy said. "We should be there in less than two hours."

Mabel felt happy riding beside her ambitious husband. His sweet potatoes were first on the market, and he had pocketed a good income from them. Last fall while cutting wood for winter, he had also cut down a long straight oak tree and drug it into the barn to dry. He used it for fuel to warm the ground for his early sweet potato plants. After the ground thawed in the early spring, he had plowed up the fall garden on the south side of the barn and with his pick and shovel had dug a big ditch across the center of the garden. Then he placed the straight tree on a bed of dry twigs in this ditch, then surrounded it with loose dry twigs and leaves that would start the log to smoldering when he lit them. After the twigs and leaves burned, it left space for oxygen to enter so the log could keep burning. On top of the log, he had placed scraps of metal that he had collected throughout the year to make a roof over the smoldering log. On top of the metal roof and many yards on either side of it, he shoveled good soil that he had prepared by mixing cow, horse, and chicken manure into the garden soil.

Inside the house Alvin grew little sweet potato plants. To start these plants, he had cut sweet potatoes in half and placed each half in a glass of water. After the sprouts grew three or four-inches-long he cut them off and placed them in containers of water. When they grew long white roots, he sold these little plants. Some, however, he planted in the warm bed he had built. All this work allowed Alvin to earn cash from the sale of the plants and to have sweet potatoes for sale long before anyone else.

Just before arriving at the drying shed in Pauls Valley, the car started sputtering as if it were out of gas. "I wonder if someone has stolen my gas?" Alvin questioned. "I had plenty yesterday." Alvin kept a clean stick under his seat for checking gasoline.

He stopped the car and stuck the stick down into the gas tank. "Plenty of gas," he said, showing Mabel the stick wet with gas. Then he checked the carburetor. "No gas," he mumbled. "The gas line must be stopped up."

Alvin worked on the motor and it started. Then they drove on to the drying shed. After unloading the potatoes, it would not start. He found a mechanic nearby who took the gas line off, cleaned it out, and put it back together. The car ran for just a short time and stopped again. The men worked on the car until afternoon, but the motor would run only a short while at a time.

When the mechanic's wife found out that Mabel and the girls had been waiting for hours, she invited them into her house. She told Bob and Dink to lie on her beautiful bed and take a nap. She gave Mabel a tin cup of cool water and asked her to sit and rest awhile. She was very friendly and enjoyed visiting with Mabel.

"We are gonna get this pretty pink bedspread all dirty," Bob whispered. "Look how dirty our feet are." Dink was too sleepy to answer.

As the hours passed, Mabel became more and more worried about Jimmy and Lois. She told the lady about her two children, ages six and eight, at home alone.

"Maybe they will go to a neighbor," she said, trying to comfort Mabel.

"I don't think so," Mabel answered. "We never thought of being away this late. It's a two-hour drive home and it's almost dark now."

Finally, just as the sun was going down, the motor ran for a long time, so Alvin paid the mechanic and they started for home. However, about half an hour later the car quit. "Do you think we may be here all night with Jim and Lois home alone?" Mabel asked.

"I'm sorry," Alvin answered. "I don't know what to do. I think God is the only one who can take care of this problem. Let's pray." Bob and Dink knelt down in the dirt and laid their heads on the running board of the car. Mabel bowed her head above them. Alvin bowed on one knee beside the car fender. He prayed first.

Then Mabel prayed, "Oh, God, please look down in mercy on us and cause this car to take us on home. Our children at home alone are most likely frightened, and Lois is probably crying. Please, hover over them and comfort them. Help Jimmy to know how to care for Lois and help Lois to obey him. Please dear Lord, show Alvin how to fix this car so it will keep running." When she finished, Bob prayed and Dink mumbled her prayer.

A few minutes after they prayed, Alvin said to Mabel, "The Lord gave me an idea. I believe something hanging on the inside of the gas line is keeping the gas from flowing. When we blow into the pipe, it goes back against the wall of the pipe; but when the liquid gas comes from the tank, something is stopping it up. I will have to loosen the pipe from both ends and wash it out from the reverse end."

There in the dark, parked beside the road, Alvin took the gas line apart and cleaned it thoroughly. He put it back together, then started the car, and he had no more trouble with the gas line.

They arrived home at about 10:30 pm. The house was dark. Before they got out of the car, the neighbor came bringing Lois and Jim.

After the neighbor left, Jim looked up at Daddy and asked, "Are you going to spank me for disobeying and going to the neighbors?"

No, son," Daddy said. "You did the right thing. Going over to the neighbors was the correct thing for you to do because you and Lois needed their care. God gave you wisdom, son."

Questions for discussions:

1. What did Alvin need to do?
2. At what time did they plan to be home?
3. What three chores was Jimmy to do?
4. Why were they late getting home?
5. Did God give Alvin wisdom to repair the car?
6. Who gave Jimmy wisdom to know what to do?

After several mechanics had worked on Alvin's car most of the day, and still it would run only a short distance, Alvin said, "I think God is the only one who can take care of this problem." He, Mabel, Bob, and Dink gathered around the car and prayed. Shortly after prayer, God quickly helped Alvin solve the problem, and they were on their way.

11 The Blizzard

. . . Whatsoever we ask, we receive of him, because we keep his commandments, and do those things that are pleasing in his sight. 1 John 3:22

"We are going to have a storm. I can feel it in my bones," Alvin said when he came in from milking the cow. "Jimmy, come and help me bring in more wood. If we get snowed in, we'll need lots of wood to keep us cozy. I cannot work in icy weather, so we will play games and read stories."

"I'll help too," Bob said.

"And me, too," Dink added.

"It's pretty cold out there," Alvin said. "Mabel, do these girls have warm coats to put on? They want to help carry in wood."

"Roberta can wear the coat, cap and mittens that Lois has outgrown. They are hanging beside the door. Dink has none; better make her stay inside," Mabel called from the bedroom where she was tacking a blanket to a patchwork quilt she had just finished piecing together.

"Okay. Bob, get on your gear, and you can come on outside to help. Dink, you stay in."

A Faithful Father

Dink stomped her little feet and made an ugly face at Daddy's back. "You better be careful," Bob warned, "you'll get some Proverbs on your behind." While Daddy was going out the door Dink stomped her feet again, but more lightly.

After they finished stacking a huge heap of wood beside the stove and more just inside the door and Daddy was taking off his coat, he said, "If it snows tonight, maybe I can get a rabbit tomorrow. They are easy to track when there is snow on the ground.

"Yummy," Jimmy said, "I like fried rabbit."

The following morning the ground was white and more snow was falling. Bob and Dink pressed their faces against the icy window and watched the bits of snow leaping and whirling in the howling wind. Snow was already banked against the tall dead grass along the fence rows. Daddy went out to check the animals. Since the watering trough was frozen on the top, he broke the ice so the cows and horses could drink. After they drank, he led them back into the warmest part of the barn. He milked the cow and laid out plenty of hay in each animal's stall just in case the snow got so deep he could not get back to the barn for a few days. Then he went to the chicken house, raked the snow away from the door, and gave the chickens food and water. He placed the eggs in his big overall pockets and went back to the house.

"There sure is a blizzard brewing," he said as he stomped snow from his boots. "I hoped to have bought winter boots and coats for everyone in my family so we could have played in the snow. However, after paying off money I had borrowed during the years of drought, there was no money left to buy boots and coats. Anyway, we are going to have fun inside, while the icicles grow long and the cold winds moan around and around our warm house." He threw Dink up over his head and asked, "Is that all right little livewire?" Dink giggled all the way down to the tip of her toes.

After breakfast Mabel got out their favorite book, *Choice Readings for the Family Circle*. Jimmy chose the first story. Then others chose their favorite. All day they stayed in the warm house while the snow kept falling. When they were tired of reading, Daddy told of fun times when he was a boy. Then they played *Hide the Thimble* and *Kitty Wants a Corner*. Mabel remembered playing *Kitty Wants a Corner* with her big Papa years ago when the snow was deep outside. Those were happy days of her early childhood among the many sad ones. She wished Papa had lived to enjoy his four grandchildren and those that might yet be born. Right then, Mabel whispered a prayer of thanksgiving to God for her happy family and for her ability to care for them. She was grateful that she was not sick like her mother had been when she was a little girl.

Toward evening, Jimmy asked, "Daddy, are you going rabbit hunting? I want a piece of fried rabbit."

"Me, too," Lois added.

"And one for me," Dink said.

"I'm sorry, but it's too dangerous to go hunting in this kind of weather," Alvin answered. "A person can get disoriented in a blizzard and freeze to death near his own home. One of these days we will buy a pair of rabbits and raise rabbits so we can have one to eat whenever we want."

Mabel treated her family to her special cornbread with sand plum jelly before they began reading again. No one wanted to go to bed, but Daddy said it was time to have evening worship. They always began with songs. Each one took a turn choosing what they would sing. Daddy then read in the Bible about how God sent a raven to feed Elijah when he was hiding in the mountains. After each one had prayed, Alvin prayed that God would supply what they needed and protect any who were out in the blizzard.

About daylight the following morning, Mabel awoke; and seeing the snow still falling, she got up and spread her new quilt over the children, put another log in the stove, and crawled back into bed. She could sleep late, since Jimmy wouldn't be going to school in this storm. Mabel hadn't been feeling very well anyway; she needed more rest. She turned over and pulled her quilt up over her ear, hoping that nothing would awaken her. Mabel was just warming up under her covers when she heard Whitey, the cat, meowing at the back door. She knew Whitey probably wanted to come in out of the cold and to drink a dish of warm milk. She tried to ignore the meowing. But Whitey did not plan to be ignored. She kept meowing until Jimmy woke and went to the door. When he opened it, he shouted, "Wow! Whitey, what have you got this time? Mama, Mama! Whitey brought us a rabbit!"

"Bring it in and close the door quickly. You are letting in the cold wind," Mabel called back. She reluctantly started crawling back out of her warm bed.

"You lie back down," Alvin said, "I'll see about that cat."

He went to the kitchen. Dink jumped out of bed and followed him. He felt the rabbit carefully to see if perhaps it had been hit by a car and had broken bones. It had no broken bones and evidently had been freshly killed, for the rabbit's body was warm. "Thank you, Jesus, for sending us the rabbit that I promised the children."

"Why you thank Jesus?" Dink asked, "Kitty cat brought it." Alvin didn't answer. He went right to work skinning the fresh rabbit, as Dink petted the cat as it lapped warm milk. He knew who sent the orders to the cat.

By now everyone was awake and up. Mabel helped the children into their warm clothes. The wind was still howling and driving snow drifts across the icy ground. The snow was so thick that they could not see the store at the end of the road, nor the neighbor's house.

"It's like we are in a white cave," Jimmy told Dink as she was watching him putting more wood into the stove.

Mama was happy to have meat, something they hadn't had for a while. She began preparing the rabbit for breakfast.

For five days they stayed inside the warm house. Only Daddy ventured outside to milk the cow, feed the chickens, and water the animals. On the fifth day the sun shone brightly, and by afternoon most of the ice on the road had melted. The next day Daddy drove into town to see how Grandma and Grandpa and Cornelius' family had weathered the storm. Cornelius had just returned from walking to the store and purchasing the things they needed. He also picked up *The Oklahoma Daily*. Alvin read the report about the blizzard in the paper.

When Alvin got home, he told them all about what he had read. "It has been one of the worst storms in history," he said, "Thousands of cattle have frozen to death. The day that the storm blew in was Armistice Day, a national holiday. It was a beautiful morning and many men went hunting. While they were out, the temperatures dropped from sixty degrees to near zero. The wind rose, causing dangerous waves on the lakes where many were duck hunting. Many little boats could not get back to shore; some capsized, others made it to little islands, but many men froze to death before help arrived."

Bob was sitting beside Daddy's knee, "I'm glad you didn't go hunting. You might have died, too," she said.

"Yes, I am too," he answered, as he rubbed his hand over her sandy-red hair. "The paper said that west of Minneapolis many cars were buried in the deep snow. Motorists all along the highways were trapped in their cars as the snow banked over them. Nearly 100 persons were stranded near New Brighton following a massive traffic accident in which 30 or more cars piled into each other. The pile-up started when a car crashed with a bus. Three more cars piled into the bus, and one of them sideswiped an oncoming car in the opposite traffic lane. Within a short time, two dozen other drivers, blinded by the snow, slid into the pile of disabled vehicles."

"I'm glad we didn't go anywhere," Lois said.

"It would be fun to be buried in the snow," Dink said.

"No, it wouldn't be fun. It would be really cold," Lois answered.

"No fun, Dink," Alvin said, and he continued telling about the storm. "The storm traveled 825 miles in six hours. There were 26.6 inches of snow in some states. God protected Oklahoma, we just got a little tip of the blizzard," Alvin said.

"I'm thankful we only got the tip, and I'm glad you prepared ahead of time and carried in the extra wood," Mabel said.

"The children helped with the wood. We worked together and trusted God to help us through this blizzard, and He did," Daddy said.

"And he gave us fried rabbit for a surprise," Jimmy added.

Questions for discussion:

1. What did God promise to those who keep His Commandments?
2. What did the family do during the blizzard?
3. What did Jimmy want?
4. How did God supply what Jimmy wanted?
5. Who protected them from the worst of the storm?

(Note: World War I formally ended at the 11th hour of the 11th day of the 11th month of 1918, when the Armistice with Germany went into effect. Therefore, it was called Armistice Day. In 1954, Armistice Day was renamed Veterans Day.)

12 Saying Goodbye to the Farm

Wives, submit yourselves unto your own husbands, as it is fit in the Lord. Colossians 3:18

"Nap time is ended," Mabel called to Lois, Bob and Dink. "Wash your faces and brush your hair while I hook Blackie to the wagon. We will get Jimmy and go to the store."

Bob and Dink climbed up into the wagon using the wooden wheel spokes for a ladder. They sat down in the bottom of the wagon where they always sat. Today Lois would sit beside Mabel on the plank seat because Alvin was not with them. "A warm spring day is a perfect day to be out and about," Mabel said. "Your daddy gave me money to buy enough flour so that I can make you big girls new birthday dresses using the flour sacks."

"Oh goodie, goodie!" Lois said.

"Maybe I can get them made before Easter if you girls help with the work that I do every day."

"We will help," they both promised.

When Mabel stopped in front of the school, Jimmy came running and stroked Blackie's face. Blackie nuzzled Jimmy. "Can we go and get a drink?" Bob asked.

"Yes, you may," Mabel answered, "while I speak with the teacher."

The drinking fountain was a long pipe with one end closed and several holes along the top of the pipe. It was hooked to a hand pump. While Jimmy pushed the pump handle up and down, water came up from the well and traveled through the pipe. When the pipe was full, water bubbled up out of the holes. While Dink, Bob and Lois were drinking, Jimmy pumped very fast, and the water shot up into their faces. "Stop that!" Lois shouted and ran to hit Jimmy. He ran away laughing. His friends laughed, too.

After picking up Jimmy, they rode on to the large store where they seldom shopped. Mabel let Jimmy hold the reins and guide Blackie.

Before they went into the store, Mama said, "You girls may choose the sacks that you would like for your new dresses."

"Really, Mama?" they both asked.

"Me, too?" Dink asked.

"It is not your birthday," Mabel answered. Bob went in and stood in front of the flour sacks stacked from the floor almost to the ceiling. How could she decide when there were so many to choose from?

Mama pointed to a sack. "I have two of this white one with flowers. I'll need one more to have enough to make a dress with long sleeves and a full skirt. Lois quickly selected that one. Roberta chose the blue one with white stars, but there were only two. "I could make a dress with white sleeves and use white for the front of the blouse. Would you like a dress like that?" Mama asked.

"Yes, Mama," Roberta answered.

Mabel counted her money. She had enough money to buy the sacks of flour. Her girls would have new birthday dresses, and she would have flour to make bread for a long time. Mabel sang happily as they rode home.

That night, after the children had gone to sleep, Alvin said, "Mabel I know you love this farm and so do I, however, I've been thinking for some time that we should leave. I told you that I found a whiskey still in the thicket down on the edge of this property. It is well hidden all right. However, the authorities could find it by tracing the smell. If it is discovered, Mr. Broady or his wife could easily blame it on me, and I might have to serve years in prison. Who would take care of you and the children if I were put away?"

"Some of those same thoughts are torturing my mind."

"It would be very easy to lay all the blame on me, since we have no money for a lawyer to defend me. Besides that, you know I have always had a strong conscience against alcohol drinks of any kind. Also, I am careful to obey the laws of our country. To make or sell liquor is illegal in Oklahoma."

"I know," Mabel said, with her head hanging low.

"There are also some other things that bother me. I'm really concerned about our children. Mr. Broady loves our children and they love him. I fear Jimmy might idolize Mr. Broady so much that he will pattern his life after him."

"Do you think Mr. Broady has that much influence? He doesn't stay around very much."

"But he will be here most every night now that he has taken a job nearby. Haven't you noticed how Jimmy follows him around?

"I hadn't noticed."

"He has a lot of influence. Another reason to leave the farm is that the government has opened up a portion of Oklahoma City to help those who lost their homes due to this recession. All we have to do is build a house and live in it, and the property is ours. This could be a chance for us to have our own home again. I could build a little house after the crops are sold and later build a nice home. A year or two later we could sell that home and buy our own farm. I think it is a great opportunity!"

"Sounds like it might be, but our whole family loves living on this farm, and these last two years you have made a good profit," Mabel said woefully. "But whatever you think is best, Alvin. I'll move wherever you wish and make the best of it, just like I did with Papa."

That summer, rains fell regularly, and Alvin made enough profit to build a house with two-room and a kitchen on a lot in Trosper Park.

Slowly, the children accepted the idea of moving; but when the day came for loading up, they were all sad. Jimmy ran to tell Blackie good-bye. The horse came galloping to the gate. Jimmy climbed up on the gate and up on Blackie's back. Jimmy reached his arms around Blackie's neck and whispered into his ear, "Good-bye, I'm going away, please don't cry," and then Jimmy laid his head against Blackie's head and cried. After sobbing a while, he wiped his face with his sleeve, and they went galloping across the barnyard. Around and around they went until Blackie's old stiff legs were wobbling and he was sweating. Jimmy was tired, too. When Jimmy got down, Blackie nuzzled Jimmy's neck as if to give him a kiss. Jimmy patted Blackie.

Roberta took Dink's hand, and they went to tell the chickens good-bye. One hen was singing, "Cluck, cluck." She had seven little yellow chicks following her. Bob picked up a chick and put it into Dink's hand. Dink squealed with delight.

Then they visited with mama cow and her calf. "Bye, bye, Moo Moo," Dink said. "We are going away." Next, the girls ran to the barn where the smell of the newly cut hay filled their nostrils. They climbed the ladder and slid down the soft mound. "Will we have another barn and hay stack like this?" Dink asked.

"No," Bob answered. "We are moving into the city."

"What's that?" Dink asked.

"It's where there are many houses close together. So close you can hear the people talking in the next house."

"Oh!" Dink said, "and where will the chickens and cows stay?"

"We aren't taking them with us. They will all stay here on the farm. Someone else will take care of them. Now let's go over and look at the watermelons." The field was full of watermelons; some were as large as a fifty-pound sack of flour.

"I want a watermelon for my birthday," Dink announced.

"I'll tell Mr. Broady. He will give you one," Bob answered.

Lois loved to play house in the smokehouse. She went there and gathered the dishes Mama had given her for playing: cracked plates, broken handled cups, and two enamel pans with holes in them. These treasures Lois put into a bucket and carried to the pickup.

One by one the children complained about moving. Mabel told each one, "God will help us. Working together and trusting in God, we will solve this problem as we have the others. God says that all things work for our good. We'll have to accept that this also is for our good."

Questions for discussion:

1. Why was Mabel happy?
2. What did she buy for the girls?
3. What did Alvin want to do?
4. Did the children want to leave the farm?
5. Did Mabel submit to her husband?
6. How were the children to accept leaving what the loved?

13 A Year of Chaos

*For whom the Lord loves he chastens [disciplines]. . . .
If ye endure chastening, God deals with you as with
sons. . .* Hebrews 12:6, 7

Before moving away from the farm, Alvin began looking for work in Oklahoma City. He would have three children in school and a new baby was coming in February. He knew a lot of people in the city, so he went among them contracting jobs for hauling coal and doing other odd jobs that needed to be done during winter.

He had kept his Reo car during those cruel years when all other matcrial goods had been snatched away. Now he needed something in which to haul coal, so he removed the trunk from his dependable car. In its place, he built a large wooden bed that jutted out behind the car, thus making it into a pick-up.

All winter Alvin used this homemade pickup to deliver coal. Through these customers, he also contracted some painting jobs which he did on warm winter days. Mabel made soup to sell. Alvin took it to different construction sites and sold hot lunches to the men. Doing these various things, he made enough money to provide food for his family and decent clothing for the three children attending Crooked Oak School. Sometimes he gave the children money to buy a bowl of chili or soup at the little restaurant across the street from the school. Bob told Dink about going into a restaurant, sitting in a booth and paying money for her lunch. Dink and Bob were sure their daddy was getting rich.

The months passed until the day for the new baby to be born. Alvin brought Grandpa and Grandma to help Mabel. The doctor came with two medical students from OU Medical Center. It was cold outside, and there were only two rooms in the house. Grandpa made Jimmy, Lois, Bob and Dink get into bed and stay there. Dink whined and fussed, but Grandpa stood beside the bed until she whimpered herself to sleep.

She awoke when she heard the doctor saying, "Another boy." In a little while, she heard Grandma squeal, "And another boy. Three sweet baby boys! They are so tiny."

Dink tried to get out of bed, but Grandpa's big hand sent her back down again. There was a lot of commotion in Mama's room: babies were crying; Grandma, Daddy, and the doctors were talking, but Dink couldn't understand what anyone was saying. After a long time, the babies stopped crying and it was quiet again. The doctor and Alvin were talking in low hushed tones. Once in a while Mama would say something. Finally, Dink went to sleep again.

When she awoke, the doctors were gone. Daddy and Bob were in the kitchen washing the dishes. Jimmy was crying. Lois was sitting in Grandma's lap, her face buried on Grandma's shoulder. Grandma's eyes were red. Dink jumped out of bed and ran to Mama. "Where's my baby brothers?" she asked.

"They've already gone to heaven," Lois told her.

"Why? They ain't lived yet."

"God wanted them," Grandma said. "They are little angels now."

"I want a baby brother," Dink said, and stomped her feet.

A Faithful Father

Mabel told Dink to sit down on the bed. She put an arm around Dink and said, "Each of us wanted the babies, however; God knows what is best. You will be much happier if you always remember that God's way is best." Dink nodded. "You will have to be my baby a little longer," she said, as she squeezed Dink tightly.

The following weeks were long and quiet. Mama stayed in bed. Grandma prepared the food and washed the clothes for the family. Sometimes Lois and Roberta helped scrub the socks and other small clothes. Alvin washed the dishes after supper with all the children helping. The lilac and scotch broom bushes were blooming, and little green peaches were forming on the peach tree in the yard, but no one seemed to notice. Usually Dink and Bob were outside playing, climbing the oil derrick, or racing in the wind, their long hair blowing straight back from their bodies; but not now, because gloom also ruled outside. Singing in family worship had a mournful note. Daddy read the Bible. Each one prayed, and if Mama was awake, they prayed around her bed. Then Grandma shooed them off to bed, and the house was even quieter and the gloom thicker.

After the spring of gloom, the hot summer came without much rain. Dust blew into the cracks of the little house. Mama was up and doing the housework now. When the wind was strong, she hung wet sheets over the windows and the doors to keep the dust from blowing in through the cracks. She covered her dishes with dish towels to keep them clean. Every clean cup, crock, pan or pail was turned upside down. Fruit and vegetables were scarce. The family had to eat dried beans, soup or grits almost every day during that hot dusty summer.

On Dink's birthday, August 25, Mr. Broady came with a gigantic watermelon. "Let me carry it," Dink begged.

"No, Dink, you can't carry it. It is almost as big as you."

"Sure I can," Dink said. "Just let me have it."

Mr. Broady placed it in her arms. It fell through her arms, hit hard on the dusty ground and busted.

"Oh, Dink, you've ruined the watermelon for your birthday. Uncle Cornelius and your cousins are coming," Mabel said.

"It's not ruined. It tastes just the same," Dink sassed back.

That night, after the cousins had gone home, Mabel and Alvin had a serious talk with Dink. Her behavior must change or Proverbs will be applied more earnestly. It did improve after that.

On September fourteenth, Dink saw a strange car stop in front of their house. Cousin Pete jumped out and came running to the door. "Uncle Alvin," he shouted, "Dad says come quickly! Something has happened to Grandpa. He fell in the doorway and he can't get up."

"Mabel, leave what you are doing and get the children in the car," Alvin demanded.

When they entered Grandma's house, Grandpa was lying on the floor at the back door. His head and body to the waist were inside the house, his legs laying limp over the outside steps. "I can't get him up," Cornelius exclaimed, as he entered the front door with two neighbors. "Maybe all four of us can get him on the bed."

With one on each side, they carried him carefully to the bed in the living room. In a few minutes the doctor came. After examining Grandpa, the doctor shook his head and said sadly, "I'm sorry, but his heart isn't beating. Even if you take him to the hospital, nothing can be done. Just as well call the funeral home."

"No. No. Not the love of my life. Jim, Jim," Grandma shrieked while shaking him. "Wake up. You can't leave us. We need you, Jim." She kissed his forehead over and over again. Then she held his hand and rubbed up and down, up and down his long arm. The doctor shook hands with Cornelius and Alvin and said again that he was sorry. Then he left.

Dink was running wild among the commotion. Alvin picked her up and sat her on a stool and said, "If you get off that stool, I will spank you." So Dink sat very quietly while people came in and out. Each one looked at Grandpa asleep on the bed, then mumbled, "That's too bad." Then they hugged Grandma, Alvin and Cornelius. Dink wanted to ask, "What is bad about sleeping? but she dared not speak. After what seemed to be a long time, Alvin and Cornelius went to the store to use the telephone to notify Uncle Jim and Uncle Aubrey. While they were gone, Dink fell asleep and was toppling off the stool, when Mabel caught her and carried her to bed. When Dink woke up, she could feel the gloom again. It was like when her little brothers became angels. It all seemed so strange. She still wondered why it was bad to sleep or become angels, but she didn't ask anyone.

Two men came in a funny black car and carried Grandpa away while he was still asleep. Bob whispered in Dink's ear, "Our grandpa will never wake up."

Dink whirled around and asked, "How you know?"

"That's what death is. Grandpa died." Dink covered her face and cried. Bob also cried. Everyone in the room was crying as the black car drove away with Grandpa.

Every day they ate together at Grandpa's house, but Grandpa was never there. In a few days Uncle Jim, Aunt Mae and Uncle Aubrey came from California. That day all the adults went away for a long time. The cousins stayed at home by themselves. Dink was afraid that Mama or Daddy might fall like Grandpa did and never awaken again. As she cried, Bob tried to comfort her.

The following day, they put on their best clothes and went together to a big building where beautiful music was playing. They had church while Grandpa lay in a box. Then all the cars lined up behind the strange looking black car carrying Grandpa in the box. They followed each other across Oklahoma City to the Moore

Cemetery. It looked like the place where Aunt Montella was taken. She was put down into a hole in the ground and left. Dink hoped they wouldn't leave Grandpa. But they did. After a lot of talking and singing, they put the box and Grandpa down in a big hole. "No, no," Dink cried. She wiggled her way through the crowd to where Mama was sitting. "Don't let them do that to Grandpa," she whispered to Mama.

"It's alright, Grandpa is not in that box. Grandpa is in heaven now."

"When did he get out of the box?" Dink questioned. Mabel put her finger to her lips. Dink knew she must not say another word.

Weeks of gloom followed just like when her little brothers became angels. Dink was still wondering why the family was unhappy because someone became an angel. Daddy cried every day. During family worship, he could hardly sing or talk without crying. When Daddy cried, Mamma cried, and Lois and Bob. Even Jimmy cried sometimes. Dink didn't cry until she went to bed. There she cried until she fell sleep.

One evening when Daddy wasn't crying, he said, "Mabel, I'm sorry for moving you away from the farm. I know you wanted to stay. Now that Dad is gone, I've been thinking about a lot of things. Maybe we should have stayed on the farm. We have had almost more problems this past year than we could handle. Forgive me, Mabel, for being afraid and not trusting more fully in God. Will you children forgive me, too?" Each one nodded. Daddy continued, "I want to make everything right, because I want God's approval on my life more than anything else."

A Faithful Father

Questions for discussion:

1. Where did the family move?
2. What did Alvin do to earn money?
3. How many little angels went to heaven?
4. Was grandpa asleep?
5. For what did Alvin apologize?
6. Why did he apologize?

After Grandpa James Alexander Hightower died in 1940, Grandma and her sons had this picture taken. They are from left to right—Aubrey Earnest, Alvin Robert, Cornelius Hall, James Ezra, Lou Ellen (Sharp) Hightower.

14 My Legs Don't Work

And great multitudes came unto him, having with them those that were lame, blind, dumb, maimed, and many others, and cast them down at Jesus feet and he healed them. Matthew 15:30

"It's time for worship," Mabel called from the kitchen door. "Jimmy, Bob, and Lois, come."

They hurried inside. They knew when Mama said it was prayer time, their Daddy was already expecting them and they mustn't keep him waiting.

When they entered, he was already singing, "O Happy Day."

Oh, happy day that fixed my choice,
On thee my Savior and my God.
Well, may this glowing heart rejoice,
And tell its rapture all abroad.

Each one sat down and joined in singing with him until the song was finished.

Oh, happy day! Oh, happy day!
When Jesus washed my sins away.
He taught me how to watch and pray
And keep rejoicing every day. . . .
—Philip Doddridge, 1755

Then they sang, "Faith is Believing," by D. O. Teasley.

Faith is believing the promise is true,
Trusting in Jesus your strength to renew;
Resting so sweetly secure on his word,
Shielded from danger with Jesus the Lord.

Faith is believing the soul's happy rest,
Faith is believing tho' sorely oppressed;
Singing in triumph whatever assails,
High on the mountain or low in the vale.

…Faith is the victory that conquers the world.…

After the songs were finished, Bob asked, "When is Dink going to be well and sing with us again?"

"I hope real soon, but unless God heals—" and Mama couldn't say another word. She was crying. Lois was also looking sad.

"You think she might never get well and die like Aunt Montella and Grandpa did?" Bob asked, in a frightened manner.

"God will take care of Dink," Daddy said, as he opened his large worn Bible. "Dink has pneumonia. Even though that caused your Aunt Montella's death, Dink is in God's hands. The doctors did all they could for Aunt Montella, but medicine can't always heal. God can heal anyone at any time. Let's read about some that Jesus healed."

He put on his glasses, cleared his throat, and read Matthew 8:14-17. *When Jesus was come into Peter's house, he saw his wife's mother laid, and sick of a fever. And he touched her hand, and the fever left her: and she arose, and ministered unto them. When the even was come, they brought unto him many that were possessed with devils: and he cast out the spirits with his word, and healed all that were sick That it might be fulfilled which was spoken by Esaias the prophet, saying, Himself took our infirmities, and bare our sicknesses.*

When Daddy finished reading, he said, "You see, Jesus healed Peter's mother-in-law. In another passage, Luke tells the stories of how he healed a blind man, a leper, and a crippled man. Let's pray that God will heal Dink just as he did those people." They all bowed on their knees. Alvin prayed for Dink. He thanked God for taking care of them and answering their prayers. Then each one prayed for Dink to get well. A few days later Dink was up playing.

A few weeks later, however, she was again sick with a fever. This time, her body temperature was higher and the infection lasted much longer. Dink talked about unreal things that she thought she was seeing. Daddy was worried. Mama was worried. They questioned, "Is God going to take our little live-wire that was constantly moving, running, skipping, climbing oil derricks, trees and most anything else? Had God decided He needed her in heaven?" These were issues that troubled their minds day and night, because Dink had been sick so many days during that winter.

When spring came, however, she was well again— running in the rain, turning summersaults, chasing the butterflies, and almost daily asking, "How many days until I get to go to school?"

"Not until September, after your birthday," Mama told her again.

"That's too long to wait. I wanna go now," she demanded stomping her feet.

Mama reproved Dink.

Later that spring, Dink took sick with another fever that lasted longer than the first two had lasted. When the fever was gone, Dink thought she would run and play again. However, when she rolled out of bed, she fell hard onto the floor. Bob saw it and called, "Mama, come quick! Something has happened to Dink."

Mama came running in and found Dink face down on the floor. "I can't get up," Dink cried out. "My legs won't work."

Mama picked her up and laid her on the bed. "Now let's try to sit up," she said. Dink raised herself up on her elbows. "Good. Now swing your legs over the side of the bed."

"I can't," Dink cried out. "I can't. Why won't my legs move?"

"Be patient," Mama said, "Being angry isn't helping."

"But I want to get up. I want to walk," Dink shouted.

Mabel sat down on the bed, pulled Dink up into her arms, and said, "Jesus will help you, and I will take you wherever you want to go. Be still. Maybe God will heal you soon from this, too, like he did when you were sick last month."

As Mabel cuddled Dink, she, too, began sobbing. Mabel knew that children all over Oklahoma City were sick with a disease called Poliomyelitis (often called polio or infantile paralysis). Many were dying. Others were kept breathing by a machine called an iron lung. Still others were losing permanent control of their leg muscles. She believed that her little Dink had the dreaded disease. Would her little Dink remain paralyzed? She also feared that because it was a contagious disease, her other children might contract it. A thousand fears plagued her mind, and yet she knew she served a God who had worked many miracles in her life. She began thanking God that Dink could breathe and that she could use the upper part of her body.

A Faithful Father

Lois and Bob gathered around Mama and hugged her. Mama tried to lay Dink on the bed again, but Dink clung to her. "Hold me," she pleaded. "Hold me tight. I'm scared."

"I need to make supper. Daddy will soon be here, and he is always so hungry when he comes home after working hard all day." She held Dink a while longer. Both were crying. Then she told Lois to come and hold Dink. Eight-year-old Lois climbed up onto the bed and Mama laid Dink's head down in Lois' lap.

When Jimmy came in and saw Mama wiping tears off her cheeks while cooking, he knew something really terrible had happened.

"What's wrong?" he whispered to Bob.

"Dink can't move her legs," Bob answered.

Jimmy went to Dink's bed. Tears were rolling off Dink's face. Lois was also crying, "Don't be afraid. You will be alright," he said.

"I can't move my legs," she wailed. Jimmy just shook his head and went back outside.

Quietness reigned in their house that night. Alvin also knew that children, not only in Oklahoma City, but in other parts of the state, were dying or becoming paralyzed after having this sickness. What did the future hold for them and their little livewire? Would they be pushing her in a wheelchair as people were doing for President Roosevelt? He was paralyzed after suffering with polio. They knew Charlotte had a lot of fight in her and she would struggle to make it through life in whatever condition polio left her. They also knew that God always has the last say. Alvin pondered: What will God say about Dink?

Mabel and Alvin's prayers that night were prayers of consecration. Alvin prayed, "Lord, we beg you to spare Dink and to heal her. That is our desire, Lord, but we submit to your will. Have your own precious way, Lord." Mabel's prayer was similar.

Day after day Mabel held Dink in her arms and tried to help her accept her paralyzed body.

Dink refused to accept it, saying, "I don't want legs that don't work. I want legs that walk and run."

"We have to accept what God does," Mabel told her.

"No, no, no, I want to run, to climb, and to walk with Bob and Lois to school."

For many months Charlotte had been asking, "How many more days till I can go to school?" Now she was asking, "Will I get well so I can go to school?"

Mabel answered, "Mama and Daddy don't know if God will heal you; however, we know He has helped us through every problem we have ever had. We will trust Him to help us through this one. His way is always best."

Questions for discussion:

1. Why did Mabel call the children?
2. What was Daddy doing when the children came in?
3. Why was Dink not worshiping with the family?
4. Did God heal the two fevers that Dink had?
5. Why did Dink fear she couldn't go to school?
6. What was Mabel's advice to Dink?

15 Does God Heal?

Is any sick among you? Let him call for the elders of the church; and let them pray over him, anointing him with oil in the name of the Lord: James 5:14

Dink awoke and heard the children playing outside. She raised up in bed but could not see out the window. "Mommy, Mommy," she called, "please take me outside."

Mabel rolled the quilt around Dink and carried her to the porch. "You can watch them playing from here," she said, spreading out the quilt so her five-year-old Dink could roll around.

Dink wriggled herself around so she could see through the banister posts. Maybe I can get on my knees and see them better she thought, so she pulled herself up until she could see over the top of the banister. "Awe," she said. But when she let go of the banister, her body fell down hard onto the quilt. She buried her face in the quilt and cried. Then beating her fists on the floor, whimpered, "I wannta go play. I wannta go play." After a little rest, she raised herself up again and watched the children until her arms were too tired to hold her body up; then she fell again onto the porch floor and cried until she fell asleep.

Sometimes Mabel carried Dink further out into the yard where she could easily watch the other children playing. She especially liked to see them dashing here and there while playing tag; however, today had been too cold to lay on the ground.

One evening during family worship, Alvin said, "Mabel, a lot of people are praying for Dink. We are committing her to God's will and being obedient to Him in every way we know; however, there is one portion of God's Word we have not obeyed."

"What is it?" Mabel quickly asked.

"I will read it to you." He put on his glasses, opened up his big Bible and turned to James 5:13 and began reading:

> *Is any among you afflicted? Let him pray. Is any merry? Let him sing psalms. Is any sick among you? Let him call for the elders of the church; and let them pray over him, anointing him with oil in the name of the Lord: And the prayer of faith shall save the sick, and the Lord shall raise him up; and if he have committed sins, they shall be forgiven him. Confess your faults one to another, and pray one for another, that ye may be healed. The effectual fervent prayer of a righteous man availeth much. Elias was a man subject to like passions as we are, and he prayed earnestly that it might not rain: and it rained not on the earth by the space of three years and six months. And he prayed again, and the heaven gave rain, and the earth brought forth her fruit.*

Alvin closed his Bible and said, "Elias was a man like me and God heard his prayers; God will surely hear our prayers, too, if we obey this commandment and send for the elders of the church."

"Yes, we must obey all of God's commandments, and that is one of them," Mabel agreed. "Also, the song, 'Obedience' goes along with what you just said. Let's sing it.

> "Dear Redeemer we will hallow,
> All thy words so firm and true.
> In thy footsteps meekly follow,
> Thy commands we love to do.
>
> Each commandment thou has given
> Is a waymark on the road,
> Leading up from earth to heaven
> To the blessed throne of God."
>
> —D.S. Warner
> —A.L. Byres

When they had finished singing, Daddy said confidently, "Jesus also told his disciples, *If a man love me, he will keep my Words, and my father will love him and he will come unto him and make his abode in him.* God has given these promises to his children, and we are his children. Another promise in John 14:13,14 says, *Whatsoever ye shall ask in my name, that will I do, that the Father may be glorified in the son. And if ye shall ask anything in my name I will do it.*"

"And Dink will be healed if we obey God and pray in Jesus name?" Lois asked.

"Yes, if it is God's will," Mama answered. "We must always stay committed to God's will. We should not command God to do what we want. I have heard people commanding God to do certain things. That is not right. We must ASK God to heal if it is HIS WILL. Your Daddy and I have been praying a lot for Dink, for she has been needing God to change her attitude. We must now allow God to do whatever he sees is best for her."

Daddy spoke again: "Each of us wants her to be running and playing again as she once did; but we must trust God's wisdom. It is difficult to say from the heart, 'Thy will be done,' when we are yearning for her to be healed; however, we must do it. We must allow God to have his way. I knew a sister in the church who had a daughter that was very sick. The mother confessed later that she did not give God freedom to have his way. God healed the girl. Later, the girl rebelled against God. She also suffered various health problems through her life. She was unable to care for herself and caused her parents many sorrows. The Mother repented for not letting God have his way when the child was young. Your Mama and I will keep Dink committed to God's will. If God heals her, we will be very happy. If God does not heal, we will accept the duty that will be ours to care for our paralyzed child as long as He chooses. If she is not healed, all of you will have to help us. Are you willing to do that?"

Lois, Jimmy, and Bob each nodded.

Then turning to Mabel, he asked, "Are you saying amen to God's will?"

While sobbing quietly, Mabel murmured, "Yes, Alvin, God's will be done."

So, then they called the Elders of the congregation where the family attended. They were Bro. Merle and McKinnly Eddens and their wives, Sis Posey, Bro. Benson, Sis. Winn, and some others. They gathered around Dink's bed and prayed for God to remove all hindrances. They asked that any sin would be revealed and confessed so the way to God's throne would be clear. After that was finished, they anointed her with oil. Then they bowed on their knees and begged God's mercy for the sick child, for her parents, and for God's divine will to be done in Dink's life.

A few days after that prayer, Dink could move her legs; a few days later she was able to stand. In a short time, she was running again. Mabel stood on the porch and watched Dink playing tag with the neighbor children in the yard. Tears of gratitude were streaming down her face.

A Faithful Father

When school started in September, Dink walked one and one-half miles with Bob, Lois, and Jimmy to Crooked Oak Elementary School and entered the first grade. At recess, she ran and played with the other children as if she had never been paralyzed.

Questions for discussions:

1. Why couldn't Dink play?
2. What commandment had her parents not obeyed?
3. Has God promised to do whatever we ask?
4. Is it important to submit to God's will?
5. Does God know what is best for each person?
6. Did God heal Dink?

The 1941 third grade class of Crooked Oak School in Oklahoma City. Roberta is sitting fourth from the right on the first row.

16 The Christmas Tree

Learn not the way of the heathen, . . . For the customs of the people are vain: for one cutteth a tree out of the forest, . . Jeremiah 10:2, 3

Mabel threw up her hands in despair and said to Charlotte, "Dink, I'm so glad you got Mrs. McIntyre for a teacher. Mrs. McIntyre will take some of this smart aleckness out of you."

Mrs. McIntyre had been Roberta's first grade teacher; and she had caused Roberta, who was already a quiet child, to become so quiet she would hardly speak. Dink was so very talkative and loved to show off. Mama thought she needed Mrs. McIntyre to calm her down, so she would have better behavior.

In September, when Mabel enrolled the children in Crooked Oak Elementary school in Oklahoma City, Jim was in the sixth grade, Lois in the fourth, Roberta in the third, and Charlotte in the first. Dink was frightened because she had heard what Mama had said about Roberta and Mrs. McIntyre.

A few weeks into the school year, Mrs. McIntyre chose Charlotte to be in the band. Only a few students from each class were chosen to be in the school's Beginners Band. She also supplied the uniform and an instrument. All through the year she treated

Charlotte with tender loving care. Some students called Dink the teacher's pet.

When school dismissed for the Christmas break, Mrs. McIntyre gave Charlotte the beautifully decorated Christmas tree that had stood in the classroom since the week after Thanksgiving. She carefully wrapped the breakable decorations and put them into a protective box so they would not get broken while carrying them home.

Charlotte walked proudly out of the room with the large shopping bag full of decorations hanging over one shoulder and dragging the tree with the other hand. She was smiling happily when she met Lois in front of the school building. She was so happy, she hardly noticed the cold wind. "Look what teacher gave me!" she said, excitedly.

"You should have told her that we don't put up Christmas trees," Lois whispered.

"But I like Christmas trees. I wanted it, it's so pretty."

"The Bible says they are idols and we should not have idols." Lois scolded.

"Look at all the beautiful bulbs and shiny tinsel." Charlotte open the sack for Lois to see. Lois turned her head and looked the other way. "At least help me carry the decorations," Charlotte pleaded.

"No," Lois said. "Look, Dink, we have a mile and one-half to walk in this storm. Don't you feel the hard bits of ice hitting on your cheeks? That big old tree will slow us down. It will take us much longer to walk home. Just leave it here."

"No," Dink retorted, stomping her feet. "Bob will help me."

"It'll be all shaggy by the time we get home. The needles are falling off as you drag it. See them on the sidewalk." She pointed to the little pine-needles that had fallen from the tree.

When Roberta came, she willingly took the bag of decorations. The heavy bag almost dragged the ground when Roberta walked. Sleet, driven by the cold wind, cut into their legs, hands and faces; but Dink felt warm and wonderful inside, for now her family would have a beautiful Christmas tree like other families.

They hadn't walked far, when a car pulled off the road behind them and honked. It was J. W. Bethel and his wife. He was a visiting minister from Oregon, teaching at the Church of God where her family attended. He called to the three girls, "Jump in and I'll take you home."

"Now, throw that old tree down," Lois reprimanded. "There isn't room for it in the car. Besides, they will think we're heathens."

"I'll walk if there isn't room for my tree," Dink said haughtily, as she pulled her coat sleeve down over her hand that held the tree.

"No you won't," Lois retorted. "We can't leave you walking alone, and it is far too cold to walk when we've been offered a ride in a warm car."

Brother Bethel settled the argument by saying, "Get in the back and hold your tree on your lap."

Because Dink was the youngest, they let her get in first. She signaled to Lois that she had triumphed and jumped into the car, pulling the tree in after her. Lois and Roberta had to squirm in under the sticker pines of the tree.

By the time they arrived at home, Charlotte wasn't so excited about her tree. Being in the presence of this minister and what Lois had said was changing her feelings. When Alvin saw it, he said calmly, "Just leave that thing outside."

Charlotte knew not to argue with him. While Bro. and Sis. Bethel and her sisters hurried out of the storm into the warm house, she reluctantly leaned her tree against the side of the house and walked slowly inside.

After the minister and his wife had gone, she asked. "Now can I bring in my tree?"

"Mama has supper ready. Let's eat now," Daddy answered. Because of the visitors, they were eating later than usual. When the meal was finished, they stacked the dishes into a dishpan without washing them, for it was then time for family worship.

Evening worship was a constant in their home. Other activities could be put aside, but not family worship. Only when they were working on the extra-long days during harvest did they tumble into bed without formal worship. Even then, Dink prayed a short prayer as she drifted off into dreamland, for prayer was the proper way of ending every day.

They all sat down in their usual places and sang a few songs. Afterward Dad opened his Bible to Jeremiah 10, and he read:

Thus saith the LORD, Learn not the way of the heathen, . . . For the customs of the people are vain: for one cutteth a tree out of the forest, . . . with the axe. They deck it with silver and with gold; they fasten it with nails and with hammers, that it move not."

He placed his worn calloused hand on the open Bible and said, "This is God's Word. These words were true when I was a little boy. They are still true. They will stand true forever. You heard me read what God said. He said that we should not learn the ways of the heathens. He also said that it is vain to cut down a tree and deck it with silver and gold. Something that is vain is useless; it has no value, so the Christmas tree has no value. Also, getting a tree and decorating it is what the heathens did. We are not heathens, we are Christians. Christians are the people who take the Gospel of Jesus Christ to the heathens. So do we want to do as the heathens do?"

"No," Lois said and gave Dink a reproving look.

That was all Dad said about the tree. Dink didn't cry or beg nor did she feel angry. She didn't want to be like a heathen. She

A Faithful Father

thought heathens were people who wore bones in their noses and ran around like animals with scarcely any clothes. And when they were hungry, they would kill and roast a helpless person and have a feast. She sure didn't want to be like them.

Dink never knew what happened to the precious tree and its decorations. She didn't really care. She wanted to please God.

Questions for discussion:

1. What did Mrs. McIntyre give Charlotte?
2. Who took the girls home from school?
3. Why did they want to ride?
4. What did Daddy read from the Bible?
5. Did Charlotte want to do as the heathens do?
6. What happened to the tree?

Charlotte's first grade class at Crooked Oak School in 1941.
Mrs. McIntyre, the teacher, was very good to Charlotte.

17 The Stolen Candy

Thou shalt not steal. Thou shalt not bear false witness...
Exodus 20:15, 16

"Dink, Bob, come inside and get ready to go to church," Mama called from the kitchen door. They continued jumping rope a little while longer. A few minutes later, Mama called again. "Dink, Bob, come in, your Daddy will soon be home and we are going to church. Hurry now! You don't have much time. You need to wash your hands, face and feet and put on clean dresses."

"Come on Dink, let's go get ready," Bob said, and started running.

Dink threw the rope over her shoulder and dragging her feet in the dust, she slowly followed Bob. "I don't wanta go to church," she complained.

"Why? You used to like to go to church. Why are you acting like this?" Bob questioned. "And you're getting dirtier. I am going to wash first, before you get your dirty feet in the water. Now if you keep kicking up dust, you may have to carry an extra bucket of water to get it all washed off. You know Mama wants us clean to go to church."

Dink was not listening to Roberta; she was replaying in her mind what had happened when Tom and Dick were staying with them:

"Let's build a playhouse out here in the tall weeds," Tom said. "Look, we can beat down the grass to make the floor, and the tall grass around us will be our walls."

"That's a great idea!" Dink answered, and they began working. Soon, a lot of space was opened in the middle of the tall grass. They gathered blocks of wood for chairs and placed an old board on top of some broken cement blocks for their table.

"Now we need something to eat," Dick said. Dink found cold biscuits and potatoes in the house, but neither food was appetizing enough for their new little play house. So she asked Mama for money to buy candy.

"Sorry, honey, I have no extra money for candy. I'll make you some lunch after a while, and you can eat it in your playhouse," Mabel promised. So Dink was contented and went back to the playhouse.

Tom and Dick, however, were not happy. "I will make some money, and we can buy our own candy," Tom said.

"You can make money?" Dink asked. "I did not know you could make money."

"Yes, I can," he bragged.

"Dick, go in the house and find me a nickel, a piece of stiff paper, a pencil, and scissors." Dink went in with Dick to find all the things they needed and was soon back with every article. Tom took the paper and pencil and rubbed the side of the lead over the paper until the image of the Indian head on the nickel was clearly seen on the paper. Then he cut it carefully around the edge.

A Faithful Father

Dink gasped in surprise. "Wow! It looks just like a nickel. Is this what they call paper money?" she asked.

"Yes," Tom answered. "That is paper money."

Dink knew paper money was good, but this did not seem like real money.

"Now let's go buy some candy," Tom said. "But first, Dick. go put this nickel back where you found it. We don't want to be accused of stealing." After Dick came out, the three started off to the store.

As they were walking, Tom said, "Dink, you are the bravest girl I know. I really like girls like you 'cause they're not afraid of frogs, snakes, climbing trees, chasing stray dogs, oil derricks, and other things that most girls are afraid of. Plus, you are such a fast runner." (Dink remembered the time when she couldn't run or walk, and now that she was able to run, she always ran very fast. She felt so happy that Tom had noticed her fast running.) He continued, "You can run faster than Dick or I, so you should be the one who goes in to buy the candy. Tell the store man that you want a nickel's worth of candy and then choose which pieces you want. When he hands you the sack of candy, you lay the money on the counter and hurry out. Now don't be afraid, it's all right, just be sure you have the candy in your hand before laying the money on the counter."

Dink's heart beat hard. This seemed like stealing. She felt like telling Tom, "No. If you want candy, you go get it." But if she did, then he would know she was afraid. She wanted to show him that she wasn't afraid just like he said. She had to do it or they would know she really was afraid. Also they might not like her if she didn't get them candy.

Dink went into the store and stood by the candy. There were shelves and shelves of delicious candy: peanut brittle, chocolates, sweet jaw-breakers, little wax bottles full of sweet drink and many others all inside a glass case. A nickel would buy a lot of candy. A sign on the chocolates read five for a penny. Even the large peanut brittle was two for a penny. The candy looked so-o-o good that Dink did just what Tom had told her to do.

"A nickel's worth of candy," she said, and pointed to the pieces she liked best. She took the sack of candy in her hand, laid the money down on the counter and hurried out. By the time old Mr. Henry was out the door, she had already turned the corner and was out of sight.

That night in family worship Dink felt heavy at heart. She could hardly sing. When it came her time to pray, she pretended to be asleep. She thought God wouldn't hear her prayers tonight, so why pray?

A few days later when Jimmy went to the store to buy an onion, Mr. Henry said. "Tell your mother that your sister came into the store and stole a nickel's worth of candy."

During family worship that evening, Daddy read the Ten Commandments and talked a long time about the evils of taking something that belonged to someone else. After prayer, he said, "Dink, Mom and I want to talk to you in our bedroom." Dink's heart was again racing; she was sure Daddy knew what she had done.

When they were in the room and had closed the door, Daddy said, "Someone told me that you have stolen candy from the store. I don't believe you would ever do such a thing, would you?"

"No," Dink said with her head down.

"For some reason you are acting like you are guilty. Did you steal candy from the store?"

"No," she answered. In her mind she told herself that she had paid for it with paper money.

Daddy took Dink's chin in his hand and said, "Look me in the eye and answer me. Did you take candy from the store without paying for it?"

"No."

The following day Mama talked again with Dink about stealing and encouraged Dink to confess if she had stolen the candy. She had already denied it to her father, so she continued denying it.

Mama was so convinced that Dink was innocent that she walked down to the store and told Mr. Henry that he must have confused Charlotte with another girl in the neighborhood who looked a lot like her.

But ever since that day, Dink had felt really bad inside. When she went to church, she felt heavy and miserable. She had stolen candy; that was a sin because she had disobeyed God's commandment: *Thou shalt not steal.* To cover that sin, she had many times disobeyed the ninth commandment: *Thou shalt not bear false witness.* She wished a thousand times that she had admitted her mistake when first asked.

Feelings of all kinds raged within Dink, but the feeling that prevailed most was the feeling that she was too guilty to pray or to ask a favor of God. How could she, a dirty sinner, touch a Holy God? How could she be part of the holy circle of worshippers? To pretend would make her a hypocrite, and Daddy had often told them the woes of a hypocrite. Thoughts raced through Dink's head as she was getting ready for church. The easiest thing to do right now was to pretend she was all right. But then a mountain loomed before her. She would have to pretend again, and again and again, on and on. It would be a never ending cycle of pretending a lie. The very thought made Dink shudder.

While waiting for her family to get ready, she covered her face in her hands and sighed, "Why didn't I admit it when Daddy asked?"

"What you mumbling about?" Bob asked.

"Nothing, nothing. Just stay out of my doings."

"You're like an old cranky bear. You'll need to repent," Bob reproved her.

"That's the problem and I can't."

"Of course you can always repent, any time, any place," she encouraged.

"Just leave me alone," Dink snapped.

So Dink went to church, but she didn't enjoy it, and she fell into bed with a heavy heart as she had been doing for the past weeks.

Questions for discussion:

1. Where was the family going?
2. Why didn't Dink want to go?
3. Why did Dink feel like a sinner?
4. Name the two commandments she had disobeyed.
5. Was she sorry she had not admitted stealing the candy?
6. What should Dink do?

This is one of the newsletters Alvin printed. Lois, age ten did the stylus work on the front page.

18 Spreading the Truth

O God, thou hast taught me from my youth: and hitherto have I declared thy works. Psalms 71:17

"I don't have to work today. Let's all work together and see if we can get some Gospel literature printed while I am here," Alvin said, as they were leaving the breakfast table.

"I have been working on the front page with the new stylus you bought me," Lois said. She brought it for Daddy to see.

Alvin looked it over carefully. "It looks wonderful!"

Lois smiled happily.

"You have done a great job! Your art teacher would be surprised that her fourth-grade student could cut a stencil so well. I like how you shaded the large block letters. Now let's see, what did we put on this page?" Alvin picked up another stencil and held it over the light table so he could read it. Lois peeked over his arm.

"That's Grandpa Kelley's article," she said. "Remember, it's mostly Bible verses."

Alvin read a few lines, " 'A WORD OF WARNING.' Let every Christian examine himself to see if he has the spirit of Christ, for the Bible says, Now if any *man have not the spirit of Christ, he is none of his.* (Romans 8:9b). If a man has the spirit of Christ, he will be like Christ, *Who did no sin and neither was guile found in his mouth.* (1 Peter 2:22). The Bible clearly teaches that Christians can live above sin. For 1 John 3:8 says, *He that committeth sin is of the devil. . .* It also says, *All unrighteousness is sin. . .* (1 John 5:17). *Beloved, follow not that which is evil, but that which is good. He that doeth good is of God. . .* (3 John 1:11)."

"See, it has lots of Bible verses," Lois said again.

"Yes, it does, and the Bible is the eternal truth that will stand forever. Now let's see what else is ready to print. Here is a testimony written by Violet Benson about her baby girl being very sick. She took the sick baby on a train to camp meeting. There the ministers prayed for the baby and the baby was healed."

"And here is one you wrote," Lois said, and began reading, "The CHURCH OF GOD of today has a message for the world. It is a God-given message of life, and just as it was in John the Baptist's time, so it is today. There are thousands of people waiting to hear this message. It is true that many will not heed even though they hear it, but it is equally true that there are those who will gladly heed the message if they know it. It is up to us, as the people of God, to take the truth to all people. Whether they heed it or not is between them and God. *Whether they hear or whether they forbear… they shall know that a prophet was among them.* (Ezekiel 2:5)." Lois finished reading and added, "This Gospel newsletter is going to be interesting."

Mabel looked up from the typewriter where she was correcting stencils and said, "Get the table cleared off so we can put the mimeograph machine on the table." Roberta, who was doing her homework at the table, gathered up her books and papers and put them on the bookshelf in the living room. Alvin spread several layers of newspaper over one end of the table, then he lifted the mimeograph out of the box where he kept it stored and set it on the paper. He cleaned the mimeograph carefully.

"It sure is a lot of work to print," Jimmy remarked. "Is it worth all the time and effort we put into it? Looks like it would be easier to just tell people instead of printing."

"We couldn't reach as many people," Alvin answered. "However, if we had equipment using the latest technology, printing could be a snap, but we don't, so we'll use what we have. For several evenings, I've worked hours and hours cutting those stencils that your mother is now correcting. And we have to be so careful and do everything so detailed. The tiniest crease on a stencil will leave a smudge mark on the printed page."

"Yes, Jimmy, it takes a lot of time and money to print these messages; but your daddy and I love truth and are willing to sacrifice our time and money to give it to others," Mabel said. "Lois also spends a lot of her time drawing pictures and headings for the front page. Printing is a meticulous job."

To cut a stencil, Alvin removed the ribbon and rolled a stencil assemblage into the typewriter. The bare, sharp, type element could then strike the stencil, removing the special coating from the tissue paper. This allowed the ink to flow through the stencil assemblage onto the paper being printed.

Mabel proofread each stencil carefully after Alvin had cut them. She brushed correction fluid over each incorrect word or letter. After the correction fluid was dry, she put a stencil assemblage back into the same typewriter, which had the ribbon removed. She would find the spot where the incorrect letter had been covered and type the correct letter or letters in its place. Then she would find another incorrect letter and type the correct letter in its place. On through the stencil she moved slowly making sure that every letter was correct. When one stencil was corrected, she would put in another stencil and correct each error. Mabel handled the stencils very carefully to avoid a crease that would allow ink to seep through making a long mark across the printed paper.

Alvin poured oil-based ink into the mimeograph drum, then he attached a corrected stencil. He placed a stack of sheet-paper behind the mimeograph and turned the handle on the drum. A sheet of paper slid through and came out on the other side with one page of an article printed on it. Lois reached for the printed paper. "Don't touch the paper until the ink dries," Daddy cautioned her. He continued turning the drum, printing one page each time it turned over. Soon he had a stack of the first page printed. He took off that stencil and laid it carefully in its place. He would use it again if he needed more prints of that page. Now he put on a stencil for the second page, and Jimmy turned the drum over and over until he had printed the number of pages needed. They did this for each page until all the pages for the Gospel newsletter were printed. When the printed letters became light, Alvin added more ink.

The Eddens and Benson families came to help mail them. Sis. Eddens, Sis. Benson and Mabel wrote addresses on the wrappers. Alvin, Bro. Eddens, Bro. Benson and the older children assembled the pages so each subscriber would receive all the pages that had been printed. The other children folded them, and the women pasted the address wrappers around some of the folded papers. Those without addresses would be given to neighbors, co-workers and strangers. Everyone worked on into the night until one by one the younger children fell asleep. When the Evening Light Messenger was finally finished, those who were awake bowed and prayed God to bless the articles to give light and hope to its readers. Then smiling with satisfaction, they carried their sleepy children to their cars and the families went home.

Mabel marched sleepy Roberta and Charlotte to their bed, and the rest of the family went to bed happy that others would also hear truth from the Bible.

A special feature in this issue would be a song Alvin had written:

> "Will You Meet Him?"
> "I can hear my Savior calling
> In a soft and tender voice.
> Come my child from sin's confusion,
> I will gladly take you in.
>
> CHORUS
> Will you meet Him in that morning?
> In that home beyond the sky?
> Will you meet Him in that morning?
> Where the soul shall never die.
>
> Mortal man why will you tarry
> See the moments flying by?
> Hear the Savior sweetly pleading
> Come to me why will you die?
>
> Oh, my child, why will you linger
> Don't you hear the spirit's call?
> Softly, tenderly He's pleading
> Come to me. Oh, do not fall.
>
> Oh, for grace that you might enter,
> Into God's beloved fold.
> Soon death's shadow will be gathering
> Around your weary helpless soul.

> If the world be cold and friendless
> Just remember Jesus knows.
> Then my brother don't be weary
> Jesus conquers all your foes."

Questions for discussion:

1. What was the family doing?
2. Why did they print the papers?
3. What did each member of the family do to help print the paper?
4. Did it take a lot of time?
5. What did ten-year-old Lois do?
6. What did they sacrifice to spread the truth?

Living in Oregon

19 A New Opportunity

Thy will be done in earth, as it is in heaven.
Matthew 6:10b

J. W. Bethel stepped out of his car and hurried toward the door of our home on Walnut Street in Oklahoma City. Daddy met him at the door and asked him to come in.

"Say Alvin, I just got a letter from my daughter in Oregon. She told me that their farm in the Willamette Valley is producing great. She also asked me to send her husband a good farmhand. I thought of you. They will advance money for the trip. Are you interested?"

"Oh! Brother Bethel, nothing could suit me better than to get my children out on a farm again. I want them to have the opportunity to grow up in a clean and healthy environment, away from the evil influences so easily found in the city; and you know I love farming. Let me talk to Mabel and pray about it."

"He needs someone really soon in order to get the land ready for spring planting, and it is already April. Let me know in a day or two or I'll be looking for someone else to help them."

While they were sitting around the supper table that evening, Daddy asked Mama, "What do you think about moving to Oregon?"

"I wouldn't mind a bit. I've wanted to go out West for a long time, and more so now that I heard my brother Albert may be living out there," Mama answered. "But with our country involved in this world war, both gasoline and tires are rationed. Do you think we could get enough gasoline for such a long trip?"

"While I'm at work tomorrow, will you see about that?"

"Sure," Mama answered.

Dink kicked Roberta under the table to show her excitement. They were not allowed to interrupt an adult conversation, so they communicated in other ways. She smiled and nodded.

That night the decision about going to Oregon was the focus of their family prayer time. Daddy and Mama each prayed, "Lord, please show us if we should take this opportunity and move to Oregon? You know what lies ahead, the dangers of traveling, and if farming out there will be profitable. You know if what we think to be an opportunity will turn out to be one or if it will be a disaster."

The children each prayed, "Please, Jesus, help us to get to move to Oregon. Please, Jesus, help us to get to move to Oregon. . ."

After they got up from their knees, Daddy said, "I think tonight we need to have a little lesson. Do you children remember when Jesus taught his disciples to pray?"

They nodded, yes.

"Jesus said that we should pray, *Thy will be done in earth as it is in Heaven.* Do you believe that in Heaven everything goes according to God's will?" They all agreed that it does. "Then we, too, must pray for God's will to be done about us moving to

Oregon." He then opened his Bible and read James 4:13-15 *Go to now, ye that say, Today or tomorrow we will go into a city . . . and buy and sell and get gain: Whereas ye know not what shall be on the morrow. For what is your life? It is even a vapor, that appears for a little time, and then vanishes away. What ye ought to say is, If the Lord will we shall live and do this or that.*

Mama added, "We should ask, if it is the Lord's will, let us move to Oregon."

Dink still wanted to move to Oregon. Bob had studied about the Oregon Trail, about the great dangers and sacrifices made on those long trips in wagons, and about the great resources found in Oregon that made all the difficulties of getting there seem like nothing. She had told Dink all about it. Dink knew they wouldn't be migrating slowly in a covered wagon. They would be traveling on smooth, safe highways in a fast car. (A car that she was sure God was going to supply.)

Jimmy had often said when he grew up he was going to live in Alaska. Through the years, Mama had searched for her brother, who had disappeared to keep from being drafted into the Civil War. She had so wished to again see her brother. Dink didn't want her brother, Jimmy, so far away that she might never see him again. She knew Oregon was north and so was Alaska. If they relocated in Oregon she would be closer to her only brother when he moved to Alaska.

Another reason for going North was to get far away from Mr. Henry's store, where she had stolen the candy. Surely, so far away, she would never again feel miserable about it. She wasn't being rebellious. She had good reasons for moving.

Early the following morning, Mama started out to find the nearest fire station, for that is where she had to apply for ration stamps which they would need for purchasing tires, gasoline and oil for the trip. Although school teachers administered the distribution of ration stamp books related to food and clothing, the fire stations were the places to obtain stamp books for tires, automobile needs, rubber footwear, bicycles, typewriters and kitchen appliances. None of these things could be purchased without authorized permission from the authorities. Mama wasn't sure if the fire station was a mile or three miles away, but she would find it. Mama really wanted to go, and getting the ration stamp books might prove that it was God's will; for without them, they could not travel.

Daddy already had a large letter "B" stuck on his car windshield. This letter allowed him to purchase enough gasoline each week to have fuel for commuting to and from his job and for driving to school, to church, shopping, etc. If he changed to a job that required more driving, he would have to fill out new papers to be able to obtain more gasoline each week.

That evening after school, they were home anxiously waiting for Mama to return with the ration books. They understood that rationing was necessary because the war must have supplies in order to win. Winning the war meant a great deal to everyone, Dink knew. They were one nation under God. "UNITED WE STAND, DIVIDED WE FALL" was a slogan they heard almost every day. No one seemed to think that rationing was an infringement on personal freedoms. Cooperating made them feel they were a part of a winning team. Children and adults alike were growing tiny gardens called Victory Gardens to help supply a little food. The children flattened tin cans, collected cardboard and newspaper and lugged them off to school. It made them feel important that they were helping win. They wanted to stop a guy called Hitler from running over all those small countries somewhere on the other side of the world. At the same time, they also were retaliating against the Japanese for bombing American shipyards away over there in the Philippines.

Every few minutes, one of the children would run outside and look down the sidewalk to see if Mama was coming.

Finally, they saw her. Bob and Dink ran to meet her. "Did you get them?" each asked at the same time.

"I filled out all the papers. We will know in a few days. The agent said he believes we will." Bob and Dink skipped all the way back to the house. Dink imagined herself a giant butterfly that would soon be migrating north.

The first thing Daddy asked when he came in from work was, "Did we get the ration books."

"I'm sure we'll get them," Mama said with a smile. "The agent was more than happy to help me. He said our country needs farmers as well as soldiers."

"Now the next hurdle is getting a more dependable vehicle," Alvin said.

"God will provide, if it is His will for us to go," Mabel assured him. "Do you think we could get a dependable one with our savings?"

"There are few cars for sale, now that our country isn't manufacturing cars," Alvin answered.

In a couple days Jim Bethel came back with Elmer Glidewell. Daddy stepped out into the yard, and the three were doing some serious talking. Bob and Dink were playing outside. They slipped closer in order to listen. They heard Mr. Glidewell saying, "I have bought a farm in Oregon and will be moving there when school is out and our home sells. I need someone to drive my pickup, because it is necessary on the farm. It is very dependable. Could you drive it out for me?"

"I would be glad to," Alvin answered. Dink and Bob hugged each other and raced into the house to share the news with Mama and Lois.

A Faithful Father

Dink knew that everything was going to be better now. From time to time, she had seen Daddy sink into his chair and sigh, "If only I could get back on a farm, I could supply better for my family." Dink thought so, too, because her daddy could do wonders with plants.

The family was poor as church mice living in a bankrupted church. But the children thought they were rich now that their family had a little savings account. Both Alvin and Mabel were full of faith. That faith spilled over onto their children. The home was filled with love, laughter, discipline and security. They worked together and trusted in God, therefore they had riches more valuable than things money can buy.

At the supper table, Alvin prayed, "Thank you, God, for this food and for providing a pickup. You have given me the desires of my heart to have a wonderful family and now, hopes of living with them on a farm. Troubled times during that Great Depression and the drought left me penniless and broken in health, but You always supplied our needs. Now You are providing much better things for us. I thank you, amen." Then he began singing, "It is joy unspeakable, and full of glory, full of glory . . ." The happy children joined in singing as Mabel served them meat patties and fried potatoes.

"Yes, God never forsakes his children," Mama agreed. "He helped us conquer the problems of those cruel years."

They all agreed. "And now we're moving to Oregon," Jimmy said, smiling.

"But how do we know we are going?" Lois asked. "We do not have the stamps for buying tires and gasoline."

"God will take care of them," Daddy answered. "He supplied a truck for moving. He'll supply other things we need."

Ignoring the fact that they had no promise of the stamps, the following day each one started sorting what they would take and what they would leave behind.

Questions for discussion:

1. What was Alvin's new opportunity?
2. What had been Alvin's desire for many years?
3. Did Alvin and Mabel want God's will to be done?
4. What should we say when telling our future plans?
5. What did Christ say about God's will?
6. Name some things God has done for Alvin's family?

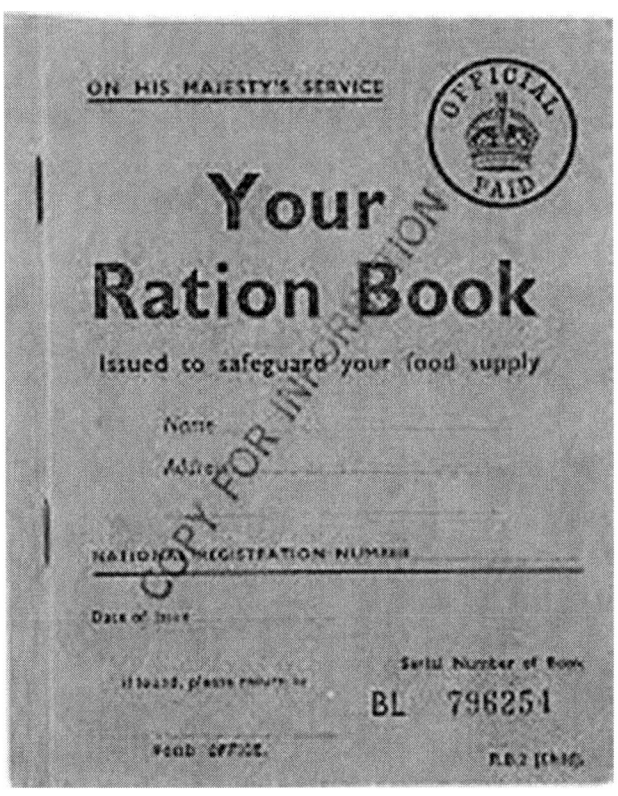

Mabel brought the ration books full of stamps and laid them on the table. During World War II, every American was issued a series of ration books. The books contained stamps for certain rationed items, such as sugar, butter, oil, canned foods, rubber and metal products. A person could not buy a rationed item without using the appropriate ration stamp. They could not have moved to Oregon without stamps to buy gasoline, oil, and tires.

20 Moving to Oregon

My help comes from the Lord, which made heaven and earth. He will not suffer thy foot to be moved: he that keeps thee will not slumber. Psalms 121:2, 3

Mabel brought the ration books full of stamps and laid them on the table. When the children came home from school, they saw the books. Bob and Dink did another little "jig for joy" then ran to their room and continued sorting their things. In one pile, they placed those things they would not take, in the other pile, the things they hoped to be taking. Bob and Dink, supposing that no toys except flat paper dolls could be taken, had already given to their church friends the few toys they owned. Joe, their rubber doll with a hole burned in his right arm, was their favorite toy, and he was still with them.

For many days, they washed clothes, sheets and quilts. Everything had to be clean to be taken or to be given away. They packed only those things that were essential, because everything they took had to fit inside the bed of a 1941 pickup. The most important things— pictures and keepsakes, Papa's lamp and his last two shirts, Mabel's childhood cup and her tiny toy iron, Grandpa Hightower's Bible and pressed flowers from his grave, the children's baby shoes and other keepsakes were placed in Mabel's big old trunk. Papa Kelley had purchased it many years ago before he and Mabel had moved to Missouri. Breakables were wrapped with small articles of clothing or newspapers to be safe on the long journey. Cardboard boxes were filled with sheets and underclothes that Mabel had made from bleached flour sacks. Dresses, shirts and pants were folded and placed in boxes. A suitcase was a foreign object. When everything was organized and packed, Mama filled her galvanized metal washtub with dishes, cooking utensils, and things they would use every day for preparing their meals while traveling.

Alvin drove up with Glidewell's beautiful pickup. It was dark blue-green with high wooden side rails that Daddy had built. Dink rubbed its smooth fenders. It felt strong. It would take them far away to the land of paradise, the Willamette Valley in Oregon—far away from Mr. Henry and fears that the truth about the stolen candy would be revealed.

The following day, they went to church as they did every Sunday. They said goodbye to Lois, John and Harry Davis, Neil and Paul Benson, and their sisters, Twyla and Margret. There was Bubby and Rosa Eddens and all their cousins, uncles and aunts. They also said goodbye to the Forest family, Sister Ank and Sister Hunter. They addressed any woman who attended church with them as Sister or Aunt. The men were addressed as Uncle or Brother.

"Remember the time your daddy was in pain and came to my house for prayer and you sat down in a hill of red ants?" Sis. Hunter asked Roberta.

Bob smiled shyly. "Yes, I do," she answered.

"Those big ants swarmed all over you. You came crying to your mama."

"Yes, I remember, not only the pain of the stinging ants, but also Daddy's pain," Bob answered. "After you prayed for him, Daddy went to sleep. I was happy my daddy was not hurting, so I went out to play." Then looking into Sis. Hunters eyes, she added, "Daddy's pain never came back."

Everybody at the church said they would be praying, so Dink knew everything would be all right. Although only eight-years-old, Dink knew that God answered the prayers of those people. She had been sick many times, and when any of them came and prayed for her, she got well.

That afternoon, Daddy, Jimmy and men from the church lifted Mama's old trunk and a tub full of breakable things up into the pickup bed. Around them, they placed cardboard boxes of clothes, an old typewriter and Daddy's printing equipment (a mimeograph machine and a gelatin duplicator). Last of all, they put the tub with dishes and pots that they would need for cooking as they traveled. On the very top, they placed two mattresses, which had been commercially cleaned to prevent carrying bedbugs into Arizona, California, or Oregon. A very large quilt (made of strips cut from the backs of Daddy's and Jimmy's old overalls) covered the mattresses and was tucked in around the sides to keep the mattresses clean. Four more quilts would be spread over the children after they were in. This would help to keep the children warm while riding in the back of the pickup for twenty-one hundred miles from Oklahoma City to Salem, Oregon. "We have forgotten one important thing," Daddy said, as he was checking over the load.

"What's that?" Jimmy asked.

"We will need the bricks that Mama puts to your feet on cold nights to help keep you children warm on the way."

A FAITHFUL FATHER

"Oh, yes," Jimmy answered. "There are some clean ones in the back yard where the girls play. I'll get some." Jimmy brought the bricks and put them inside the tailgate.

"We must remember to take these in each night and let them heat overnight in the stove oven, then they should stay warm for several hours," Daddy said.

A large canvas tarp was thrown over the entire pickup bed and secured tightly at the bottom of the wooden rails. It looked much like a covered wagon on wheels. An opening in the front of the canvas made it possible to look through the back window of the pickup or to notify their parents of any emergencies that might arise.

Only one child could ride in the cab between Mama and Daddy. Three children would have to snuggle up under those covers to keep warm through wind, rain, and snow as they sailed along the highway traveling almost 40 miles an hour.

Bob had carried Jo in her arms all afternoon as she watched the men loading the pickup. Now, she needed to part with her favorite doll. She could see her best friend, Susana, jumping rope in her yard. Slowly, Bob walked to the neighbors, she placed Joe gently into Susana's arms. "I'm giving Joe to you. Please do take good care of him," Bob begged. Then she ran back to the far side of the pickup so no one could see her crying.

In a little while, Dink said to Daddy, "We want to ride back here." She crawled up onto the bed. Bob followed her. Dink spread paper dolls out and Bob tried to play, but tears kept dropping on the paper dolls. Mama and Lois were sweeping and mopping the house, leaving it clean for the next renters. Dink and Bob had already finished their work of gathering up trash, washing windows, raking the back yard and sweeping the bare front yard.

Susana was holding Joe when they waved goodbye to her and the neighbors who were standing around. Then they drove to the Glidewell's home, where they were to spend the night. Sister Glidewell had supper on the table when they arrived. Daddy and Brother Glidewell discussed the trip while they ate. "I think you best go through New Mexico, Arizona and California," Bro. Glidewell said. "You might get into a bad snowstorm going through Colorado."

"That is how Mabel and I had planned," Alvin agreed, "for we wish to stop a few days to visit my mother and my brothers, Jim and Cornelius, who live in Los Angeles. That will also give the children a rest. They'll be pretty tired of being cooped up for three days." After more discussion and instructions about the pickup, Alvin said, "We'd best be getting off to bed; 3:00 a.m. will come mighty soon. We want to leave by 4:00."

When Dink awoke the following morning, the room was very bright. She nudged Bob, "Wake up, it's snowing." The girls looked out. Things outside were covered by a blanket of snow, and icicles were hanging from the roof, the telephone lines and trees. Daddy heard the girls talking and came to the door. "The windchill factor is well below zero," he said, "I didn't wake you, because we cannot travel until this blizzard blows away."

The blizzard lasted three days. By the evening of the fourteenth, the frozen streets had thawed enough for safe traveling. Before daybreak on the 15th of April, Sister Glidewell prepared pancakes, ham and eggs. After they had eaten, Alvin read Psalms 121:1-8, *I will lift up mine eyes unto the hills, from whence cometh my help. ... Behold, he that keeps Israel shall neither slumber nor sleep. ...The Lord is thy keeper: The Lord is thy shade upon thy right hand. ...The Lord shall preserve thee from all evil: he shall preserve thy soul. The Lord shall preserve thy going out and thy coming in from this time forth, and even for evermore.* When Alvin finished reading, the two families knelt and prayed for protection on the long journey.

When all the goodbyes were said, Jimmy, Bob and Dink, clad in coats, stocking caps and long heavy stockings, crawled up onto the bed in the back of the pickup. Each child carried two warm stones wrapped in newspaper. They crawled onto a warm quilt Daddy had already spread to protect them from the icy-cold mattress. Then three other warm quilts were spread over them. Lois sat between Mabel and Alvin in the warm cab.

The dark green pickup hummed a merry tune as it carried the happy Hightower family toward Oregon, where hundreds of Easterners had found success farming or earning fortunes working in the shipyards in Portland.

They traveled on the smooth cement highway # 66. Building this wonderful new highway had been one of the Government's projects that helped men to keep food on their table during the painful years of the Great Depression. Droughts during the dust bowl days had removed most all vegetation from the land in this area. For hours and hours, they drove through flat, lifeless land.

However, in the late afternoon, Dink peeked out and saw what looked like a giant brown teepee rising up against the sky. "Look! Look!" She cried, her teeth chattering. "Is–is–that a mountain?"

"Must be–be," Bob answered, trembling in the wind from the crack in the tarp where Dink was peeking out.

"It is the Tucumcari Peak, a real mountain all right," Jimmy answered. "It's almost 5,000 feet high. But get the tarp closed! You're freezing us."

"Wee!" Dink whistled.

Just before dark, they stopped beside a row of tiny houses standing side by side like a row of tin soldiers ready to march. Daddy rented one for the night. Bob and Dink dashed in. "It is warm in here," Bob said, as she held her cold hands over the stove. It was one big room with two beds, a cooking stove and a table with chairs. The sheets on the bed were of fine, smooth material, white as snow. They were very different from their sheets that Mama had made by sewing bleached feed sacks together.

While Jim held up the mattress, Daddy fetched out the big iron skillet and a tall soup kettle with a slab of salt pork, potatoes, carrots and onion in it. "Here, Lois, carry this in," he said, handing her the pot. Then he handed out a mixing bowl containing flour, baking powder, salt and lard. Mabel carried it in.

While the soup was cooking, Mama mixed up biscuits and cooked them on top of the stove in the big iron skillet that had a heavy iron lid. After eating, they sang a few songs and prayed. It had been a long, cold day. The warmth in the room caused them to be sleepy; but before going to bed, Daddy and Jimmy went to the pickup and brought the quilts and the stones inside so they would be warm the following morning. Then they settled down quickly for the night.

The following day, when Alvin stopped to put gas in the pickup, Dink opened the tarp just a little and peeked out. The earth shot up from the ground like a wall. She crawled to the other end of the pickup and peeked out. It looked the same. The sides looked the same, too. "It looks like we are inside a giant bowl! What are those huge rocks all around us?" she asked.

Bob shrugged her shoulders. "I don't know."

Jim, who was five years older and knew everything, said "Those are the Sandia Mountains. We are coming into Albuquerque. We passed a sign that read Albuquerque Basin. But leave that tarp down!" he demanded. "It's cold."

Dink looked at Bob and said, "Oh, I thought all mountains looked like Indian tepees."

"Yeah, like the one we saw last night," Bob said. Jimmy laughed, but not his usual hardy laugh. He was too cold. Snow was falling again.

A Faithful Father

Questions for discussion:

1. Why were the stamp books important?
2. What vehicle did God supply for them?
3. Why did Dink believe everything would be fine?
4. How do we know it was God's will for them to move?
5. What did they do every evening before going to bed?
6. Name some ways God helped the family?

21 A New World

The Lord shall preserve thy going out and thy coming in from this time forth, and even for evermore.
Psalms 121:8

Every night they rented a warm, one-room house and carried in their cooking utensils, quilts, and bricks. Mabel cooked hot soup and baked bread, while the children did jumping jacks and other exercises to burn up their energy. Every morning before leaving the little houses, Mabel fried salt pork and a dozen eggs and baked enough bread for breakfast and lunch. She had tucked in jars of homemade jelly, which they smeared over the hot bread. Sometimes she boiled another dozen eggs to eat with their biscuit sandwiches.

The day before, at about noon, they had taken out the salt pork sandwiches and eaten at a roadside picnic table. It was cold, but Alvin believed in sitting down and eating reverently. He treated food as if it were sacred, and eating, almost like a religious act— maybe because he had endured many hungry days during the Great Depression, or maybe because he knew only God could make food to grow. But today, icy wind lashed Daddy as he came around the pickup. He handed Jimmy, Roberta and Lois each

A Faithful Father

a sandwich and a quart jar full of water to share. "We will just drive on instead of getting out in the cold," he said. His teeth were chattering. Wind was driving the heavy snow almost parallel to the earth.

Nearing an inspection station at the border of Arizona, Alvin pulled to the shoulder of the highway and bowed his head. "Oh Lord, the inspection station is ahead. Please help the men to have mercy on us, dear heavenly Father. We have nothing to hide. We are obeying all the laws that we know. Please, don't allow the inspector to force the children to get out and stand in this blizzard while he inspects our load."

Mabel prayed, "Yes, Lord. We are at your mercy. Please do protect our dear children, who can barely keep from freezing under their quilts. Please don't allow them to get more chilled."

A few minutes later, they arrived at the inspection station. Alvin stopped and again bowed his head. Mama praying all the while, watched from her window for the man on duty to come out. He did not come out to inspect. They waited. They waited longer. After a while, Mabel saw the office door open, just a crack, and a gloved hand came out. "He's waving like he wants us to move on!" she shouted. The pickup rolled ahead and stopped again. "He's waving again," she said. "Let's go!"

A few miles ahead, Daddy stopped again and they bowed their heads. This time, Mama prayed. "Thank you, Jesus, for hearing our prayers and doing even more than we asked. None of us had to get out in the cold!"

Alvin knew the children riding in the back of the pickup were very cold; so, earlier than usual, he rented another little one room house. It was warm inside. Soon Jimmy and the girls were laughing again. With a full tummy and a warm bed, sleep was sweet.

It snowed all night. Discouragement showed in Alvin's and Mabel's faces. Their prayers were extra long that morning. They pleaded with God to keep the children from getting sick, for His protection through the blizzard, and that the weather would change.

Alvin carried out the warm quilts and stones in lashing, icy wind. The girls had been taking turns riding in the cab. Bob got into the warm cab. Then, one by one, the other three children—Lois, Dink and Jimmy climbed into the back of the pickup. They were stiff with cold by the time they snuggled together under the four warm quilts. Each child hugged a warm stone to his body, and Daddy placed three other stones at their feet.

By about noon, they drove into the sunshine. The blizzard was behind. Soon, they arrived in sunny California. They had read Grandma's letter about California, "No ice, no snow. Never is cold," she had written. What fun to peek from under the tarp at all the strange sights.

In Oklahoma, and Texas, the ground was bare and lifeless; in New Mexico, they saw mountains, and in Arizona, they had passed through forests of Christmas trees—giant ones, covered with snow. In California, some of the trees were tall like telephone poles with branches at the tops. They looked much like umbrellas or string mops turned upside down. They passed dry bushes without any leaves. There were lots of dead looking branches covered with thorns poking up out of the ground. Dink wondered why they didn't blow over, since they were dead. Others looked like the tops of huge pineapples. Everywhere they looked, they saw strange plants growing in soft sand.

Nearing the metropolis of Los Angeles, they saw businesses of all sorts and houses stacked on houses up the sides of hills. Cars and people were hurrying this way and that. Daddy stopped to wait for green traffic lights every few minutes. Since it wasn't so

A Faithful Father

cold, they could peek from under the tarp and see it all plainly. Even the people looked and dressed differently. Their friends in Oklahoma had either black or white faces. Here, they saw people with light brown faces and others with yellowish skin and small eyes.

By evening, they were at Uncle Jim Hightower's home. His house on a hill loomed up before them like a castle. It was big and white and sat up on a hill. Many wide stairs led to its large glass front door. Roberta, Jimmy and Dink climbed out of the pickup and stretched in the warm sunshine. Mama tried to brush out the wrinkles in their dresses and smooth down their fuzzy uncombed hair. When Dink complained, she said, "I'm trying to make you more presentable." Bob and Dink held hands and counted the stairs as they went up.

Behind the house, a huge wall of earth rose almost vertically. Someone had cleared away enough so that the backyard was about 15 feet deep and a little wider than the width of their house. There was a big stone fireplace in this small yard. They called it a barbecue pit. "This fireplace must be used to warm up the little back yard when it snows," Dink whispered to Bob.

"Don't you remember Grandma's letter?" Bob reminded her. "Grandma said it never snows here."

"Then I want to live here," Dink replied.

Grandma, Uncle Cornelius and his seven children also lived in the Los Angeles area. They came over to visit. That evening, Uncle Jim built a fire in the fireplace that they called a barbecue pit and cooked wieners and meat patties. Uncle Jim called the wieners hot dogs. "How's come you called them hot dogs?" Dink asked. "Are they made of dog meat?" Her family sometimes ate, rabbit, coon, and opossum. Some of the neighbors thought that was strange, and Grandma Josefina served fried cat to her slave master. But

Dink had never heard of anyone eating dogs. Neither did the meat patty he called hamburgers taste like ham that her mama cooked.

For three beautiful sunny days, they played again with cousins Tom, Bill and Dick. It was fun in the day; but when all was quiet at night, Dink remembered the candy that she had stolen when playing with them so long ago in Oklahoma. It made her unhappy.

They left Los Angeles so early that the sun was hidden. They traveled all day, arriving in Sacramento just before dark. "Bro. Bethel has already rented a house for us in Oregon," Daddy told Mama, as they were settling into another little one-room house that evening. "Lord willing, we will be sleeping in that house tomorrow night."

"I do hope so," Mabel answered.

"There are a lot of mountains between here and the Willamette Valley," Jimmy said. "We may have to drive slowly through the mountains."

"We will make it through. We are trusting in God and working together the same way we have conquered every problem until this day," Alvin reminded Jimmy.

"Will we get into snow again?" Lois asked. "I don't like driving in snow. It's scary."

"It's not scary, it cold," Dink interjected. "Too cold."

They did not get to the house that Bro. Bethel had rented that evening. They slept in another little one-room house. It was surrounded by giant Christmas trees. "This is like fairly land," Dink said, as she and Bob were gathering pine cones that had fallen from the trees. Jimmy tried guessing the height of the trees and estimating the size of their trunks. Lois helped Mama make supper.

They fell asleep to the sounds of wind singing through the tall trees.

A Faithful Father

Questions for discussion:

1. What did Alvin and Mabel ask in their morning prayer?
2. What happened at the Arizona inspection station?
3. When did they get out of the blizzard?
4. Who did they play with in Los Angeles?
5. What did Dink remember when playing with her cousins?
6. Did they get to their home in Oregon?

On their way to Oregon, Alvin's family visited his brothers in Los Angeles. Here they are pictured with his brother, James and wife Mae, and Grandma.

22 An 'Old Timer' House

He has brought us into this place... and thou shalt rejoice in every good thing that the Lord thy God has given thee.... Deuteronomy 26:9, 11

"Here is our home in Oregon," Alvin announced, when he stopped in front of an old two-story, weathered-gray house. "Bro. Bethel led us right to it."

Jim Bethel stepped out of his car and said, "The house is open. Wife came over and cleared out the dust and cobwebs, so it is ready to live in. Every Friday night there is an auction in Stayton, a town east of here. It's a good place to buy things you'll need. We bought a cooking stove, table and chairs there, and I have already put them inside the house. Do you have the other things you need?"

"Yes, I think we can make do. We have two mattresses and our bedding; also, we've been cooking our meals along the way. We can use those things for a while. Thank you for getting the house ready," Alvin answered, as he was unhooking the tarp over the pickup bed. "I will pay you as soon as I get to working."

All the way to Oregon, Bob and Dink had pretended they were traveling in a covered wagon. When the weather was warm and Daddy wasn't driving very fast, Dink stuck her hand out and patted the side of the pickup to encourage her imaginary horses. When Jimmy would allow them to open the tarp, they fought with make-believe Indians racing along their side. Jimmy wasn't for foolishness that made him cold, so most of their pretending was done inside; but at last, they had arrived at the end of their Oregon Trail.

As soon as the men had gone inside, Bob and Dink jumped out and raced into the house. "Look! Look! It is an old timer's house with a stone fireplace," Dink shouted.

"It's just like the Pilgrims had, where they roasted their turkey for that first Thanksgiving," Bob said quietly. "Maybe we can roast our Thanksgiving turkey here."

"And look, a dark scary stairway behind the chimney. We never had a house with stairs. Do you think ghosts hide under that stairway?" Dink asked.

"There is no such thing as ghosts," Bob answered. "But let's go up to see what's up there." She started up. The old stairs creaked under her weight. "Look, the fireplace is up here, too, and a little fence to keep us from falling down the stairs. I can see you coming up."

Dink looked up and saw Bob looking over the fence. She hurried up and opened a door at the top. "Here are two rooms behind this door, a little one and a big one. I get the little one 'cause I'm little," she said.

"There is only one room over here," Bob said, as she opened another door on the other side of the stairway. "But it has two windows, one toward the north and the other one opens where the sun comes up."

"How do you know where the sun comes up away out here in Oregon?" Dink asked.

"It always comes up in the East."

"But east in Oklahoma might be over there and east in Oregon over here," Dink said, throwing her hands this way and that.

Bob just shook her head. "This is no time to argue about the sunrise; there are too many things to see." They dashed down the hall beside the stairway fence into another big room.

"Look at this room! The tree branch comes right up to the window!" Dink shouted. "We could climb out the window and into the tree." She started trying to open the window.

"Don't do that or you will get us into trouble, then we can't keep exploring," Bob scolded.

"Come on let's go down and out on the porch," Bob called from halfway down the stairway. "Look! It has the neatest water faucet," Bob said, when they were on the porch. "Instead of turning a knob, you lift this long handle up and down and water comes out." She moved the handle up and down quickly, and water came out a little spout.

"Let's go see the barn," Dink called as she raced away. They climbed the ladder onto the loft, jumped into the soft hay, and slid all the way to the floor. They did it again and again. She really felt like a butterfly that had migrated north in her cocoon and now she was free! She was far away from Mr. Henry's store where she had stolen the candy. He would never find her a way out here.

"This barn is like our barn on the farm in Oklahoma. But what was the big building we ran past on our way to the barn?" Bob asked.

"I don't know," Dink answered

They ran back to the big building and peeked in. "Nothing but wood in it," Dink said. Just then, Jimmy showed up.

"This is the woodshed. We will be cooking meals and heating the house this winter with wood."

"Just like people did in the olden days," Dink said, as she danced around. "We are truly old-timers, just like Mama reads about in our books."

"Yeah, we are gonna live like old-timers all right," Jimmy added. "We will be splitting and carrying in wood every day. And did you notice this house has no lights? There is no electricity in it."

"How we gonna see at night?" Dink asked.

"We'll have lamps like Grandpa's old lamp that Mama keeps in the trunk. They have oil in the bottom and a little wick that burns the oil. There is one sitting on the table."

They ran in to see the lamp on the table, and that is when Daddy called, "Everyone come and help unload. It will soon be dark, and we have no lights to work after dark."

"I'm coming," Jimmy answered, "as soon as I get a fire built so Mama can get supper started."

Dink carried in the big pot that they had used every day on the trip. She watched Mama getting water from the strange faucet on the big back porch.

"Where does the water come from?" Dink asked, while she was helping Mama wash and peel potatoes in the wooden sink under the strange faucet.

"This is a pump," Mama said, putting her hand on the place where the water came out. "There is a well under this pump and water comes up through a pipe. See the pipe under the sink?"

Dink peeked under the old wooden sink. "This is a funny kitchen," she said, as she ran her fingers along the moss-covered sides of the rectangular sink. A V-shaped trough made of two boards wired together carried the water away. The wastewater ran out a little hole in the bottom of the strange sink and into this trough. She watched the water flowing into the yard near a firebush covered with red flowers. "Can we wash dishes out here?" she asked

"In warm weather during the daylight you can bring the dishpan full of hot soapy water out here and wash the dishes," Mama answered.

Jimmy, Bob, and Lois were busy helping Daddy. They put the boxes of clothes into the big cedar-lined closet between the large bedroom and the kitchen/dining area where the table and cooking stove were. Daddy's printing equipment and a box of books were placed in the corner of the big room near the stone fireplace. The tubs and boxes of dishes were placed in the pantry. One mattress was laid on the floor in front of the fireplace and the other in the large bedroom.

Before dark, the pickup was empty, and they had found night clothes and sheets and quilts for the two beds. Jimmy took his quilt upstairs. He wanted to sleep in his new bedroom. He had never had a room all to himself.

Mabel lit the oil lamp and placed it on the dining table. They gathered around the table and ate the potato soup and cornbread she had made. "Everything is in place for the night because everyone was helping," Mabel said, "but it is too dark to wash dishes. We will wash them in the morning."

"Can we wash them outside in the wooden sink?" Bob asked.

"We will see about that in the morning," Mabel answered.

During worship, the girls sat on the mattress in front of the fire that Daddy had built. Jimmy sat cross-legged on the floor. Daddy brought chairs from the kitchen for Mama and him. Lois found the three song books. She passed one each to Mama and Daddy and sat down beside Bob to share the other book. "I want to sing, "Jesus Is Good to Me," she said.

"Jesus Is Good to Me"

Jesus has been so good to me,
No other friend so kind could be,
Safely keeps me every day,
Free from sin and in the way.
Ne'er can I such love repay,
He's so good to me.
  —D.O. Teasley

After singing "Jesus is Good to Me," they sang "The Happy People," written by D.S. Warner and B.E. Warren.

"The Happy People"
Who but the Christian is happy and free
Filled with the glory of God?
None in creation so happy as he,
Washed and redeemed in the wonderful blood.

Jesus the one who my sorrows hath healed,
Thou art the one who my spirit has sealed.
Only thy glory from heaven revealed,
Only thy favor can happiness yield.

When they finished singing, Daddy held his big Bible close to the soft light of the little oil lamp and read Psalms 18:18-24:

They prevented me in the day of my calamity,
But the Lord was my stay.
He also brought me out into a large place;
He delivered me because He delighted in me.
The Lord rewarded me according to my righteousness;
According to the cleanness of my hands
He has recompensed me.
For I have kept the ways of the Lord,

> *And have not wickedly departed from my God.*
> *For all His judgments were before me,*
> *And I did not put away His statutes from me.*
> *I was also blameless before Him,*
> *And I kept myself from my iniquity.*
> *Therefore, the Lord has recompensed me according to my righteousness,*
> *According to the cleanness of my hands in His sight.*

"Children, God protected us on the long trip just as he protected David when King Saul was trying to kill him. Driving on snowy, icy highways, over steep mountains, and meeting other cars face to face is very dangerous. But God helped us and brought us safely to this beautiful land. We have tried our best to obey all of God's commandments and to let him have his way in our lives. He has rewarded us by bringing good to us. Let us be very thankful for all His blessings."

After prayer, Daddy and Mama went to their room. Jimmy went upstairs to his room. Lois, Roberta and Dink lay on their stomachs and watched the sparkling fire. "I like living in the olden days," Dink said, as she drifted into dreamland.

Questions for discussion:

1. Who brought them safely to Oregon?
2. In what are they to rejoice? (verse)
3. What song did Lois want to sing?
4. Did the family obey God's commandments?
5. For what was God rewarding them?
6. Would you like to live in a house like theirs?

North Santiam School in 1947. These are all the students enrolled in the sixth, seventh, and eighth grades. Wow! What a little school.

23 A Little School, A Big House

The foolishness of God is wiser than men: and the weakness of God is stronger than men.
1 Corinthians 1:25

Monday morning Mabel walked with Jimmy, Lois, Bob and Dink down the gravel road to the North Santiam School. North Santiam consisted of the school, a general store, owned and operated by Mr. James, and houses scattered among the farms in the area. The school building had two classrooms and a small kitchen. In recent years the number of students had increased, making it necessary to hire a third teacher, Mrs. Scofield. She instructed the fourth and fifth graders in the kitchen area. Jimmy was in the eighth grade, Lois was in sixth grade, and Bob, finishing fifth. Dink was in third grade, so she was added to Mrs. Wheeler's class of first, second, and third grade students.

The school in Oklahoma City taught cursive writing in fourth grade, so Dink, in the third grade, wrote manuscript letters. Dink wrote her spelling words in manuscript letters. Mrs. Wheeler marked every word with a red X and returned the paper with a big "F" scrawled across it. Each time Mrs. Wheeler returned Dink's papers, she said, "I accept papers only in cursive." This happened to every paper Dink turned in. Dink went home crying day after day. She whined and fussed about it until Mabel walked down the road to the little school and explained to Mrs. Wheeler that the schools Dink had attended did not teach cursive in the lower grades, therefore Dink did not know how to write in cursive. Mrs. Wheeler's response was, "She's a big girl, she can learn."

Lois also met with problems and was put back into the fifth grade with Roberta. Mabel felt sorry for the girls, but she could not solve their problems, so she prayed. The next time they came home crying, she talked to them while they were preparing supper. The girls were peeling potatoes and she was making hot rolls.

"Girls," she said, "education is very important. I had very little opportunity to go to school. I have always wished I had more schooling. However, God has given me wisdom to do whatever I have needed to do. God's wisdom is far superior to man's wisdom. Remember to ask God to give you wisdom and to help you to know how to use it. By trusting God for wisdom and using it, you can master your difficulties."

Then turning to Roberta, she said, "Go get your daddy's Bible and read Ecclesiastes 2:26. Bob read from the Bible: *God giveth to a man that which is good in his sight, wisdom, and knowledge, and joy: but to the sinner he giveth travail, to gather and to heap up, that he may give it to him that is good before God....*"

"Now turn to the book of James and read chapter one, verse five." Bob read, *If any man lack wisdom, let him ask of God who giveth to all men liberally and upbraideth not, and it shall be given to him.*"

"Our family works together and trusts in God; that is how we conquer every problem. Never forget it."

There were also problems adjusting to the house they rented from Mr. James. It was old, maybe 100 years old, and mysterious.

A Faithful Father

The first few weeks at night they felt eerie going up the long creaking stairs in the dark. Dink trembled when she remembered the stolen candy, but she was too ashamed to admit it.

As they got accustomed to the long, creaky stairway and spent hours swinging on the tire swing that Daddy had hung from the Maple tree in the backyard, feelings of warmth and happiness replaced the eerie ones. When they laughed, their laughter echoed back from the high ceilings. In the winter, they sat in front of a crackling fire and played checkers or sang together. Sometimes they went to the upstairs balcony and sat with their backs against the warm stones of the chimney while Bob read to Dink. Lois listened while she sketched pictures.

Moss grew on the roof, and mossy dormer windows peeked to the outside. There were three covered porches. The one on the north covered the two front entryway doors; one door opened into the living area and the other, into the dining/kitchen area. The porch on the east sheltered another outside door. An upstairs window opened directly above it. Dink loved to climb out the window, sit on the roof in the morning sun, and wiggle her toes down into the soft green moss on its roof.

The south porch was the largest and used for many activities. Friday evening and Saturday, they did laundry on this porch. When they came home from school on Friday, they gathered up all the dirty clothes. In a large tub, they put Jimmy's and Daddy's overalls and other dark clothes. White and very light colored clothes were placed in another large tub. With a knife, they shaved slivers of lye soap from a bar and scattered them over the two tubs of clothes, then they pumped buckets and buckets of water and poured the water onto the clothes. All the socks were put into a bucket because they were always very, very dirty, and this dirt had to be scrubbed out before putting them with the less soiled clothing. The clothes soaked all Friday night.

All day Saturday they took turns rubbing each piece of clothing back and forth, back and forth on a tin rub board until all dirt and stains were out of the cloth. While one girl was scrubbing, the other girl filled another tub with clean water and be dunking the clean clothes up and down in the clean water to rinse them. Another, would be rinsing the dirty water from the bucket full of socks. Then she would rub each sock with the bar of lye soap and put them to soak in clean water.

Sometimes they swished the clothes in the water, pretending the tubs were oceans and the clothes were great ocean liners traveling to faraway countries. "Mine is going to Ireland," one would say. Another answered, "Mine's off to India."

Sometimes Dink imagined the socks were ducks. "Look, my duck just caught a fish," she would call to Bob, while quacking like a happy duck.

In the summer, after the clean clothes were hanging on the lines to dry, they were allowed to splash each other with the cool water. Sometimes they chased each other with buckets of water. When Mabel thought they were getting too wild, she would call, "It's time to take your baths and get ready for Sunday School tomorrow." By that time, they had forgotten their tired muscles and aching backs.

In the winter, they washed clothes near the cooking stove in the kitchen and hung the wet clothes on lines strung about two feet apart back and forth across the south porch. The porch roof protected the clothes from rain that fell almost every day.

Spring, summer and many days in the fall, they washed dishes on this porch. They heated water in a large teakettle on the kitchen stove and carried it to their dishpans, which they placed in the big wooden sink. They also washed, peeled and chopped vegetables and fruit out there.

Alvin repaired inner tubes when their car had flat tires. He sharpened knives, hoes, shovels and other tools. They washed mud off their shoes and boots and did many other things. Besides the kitchen, this porch was the most used part of the house. Dink and Bob loved doing jobs outside on this porch.

Large windows in every room helped Alvin's family tolerate the long, rainy winters. They were accustomed to sunny, windy Oklahoma City.

Electricity was not available in rural areas when the old house had been built. In 1943 when the Hightowers moved into the house, it was available only to farmers with electric motors used for irrigating crops

Mabel bought kerosene oil lamps. Each evening at dusk, they filled the lamps and cleaned the glass globes. To clean the globes, they rubbed off the soot with newspaper, then they washed them with soapy water and dried them until every water drop had disappeared. Using scissors, they trimmed the black from the wicks, shaping them into a kind of dome. If the wick had pointed edges, it would blacken the globe quickly. Dink loved the soft glow of the oil lamps.

The house had no inside bathroom. Day or night, sunshine or rain, they had to walk out the back door past the woodshed and the rabbit hutches to the tiny outhouse

Alvin and Mabel went to the auction almost every Friday night. They bought many things for the house: beds, chairs, boxes of dishes, tools, glass jars, etc. They bought boxes that had something they needed in them and underneath that, they often found surprises. Bob and Dink got up early on Saturday mornings to be first to find these treasures. A few times, Alvin and Mabel took the girls. It was so exciting to hear the auctioneer talk so loud and fast. "How do you know what he is saying?" Dink asked Daddy.

"You have to listen carefully," Daddy answered. After many trips to the auction, the old house became a home.

After Mama had talked to the girls about God's wisdom, she kept praying for them. Charlotte discovered a way to change her manuscript letters into cursive letters. She first wrote straight separated manuscript letters, then she went back over every letter and drew short lines connecting the letters in each word. Sometimes she had to work during recess to get her work done, but Mrs. Wheeler marked no more "F's" across her papers.

Lois also soon adjusted to the change. She was happy with her new teacher, Mrs. Schofield, for she gave Lois individual attention that Lois needed and did not get in the large schools she had attended before.

Living without electricity or inside plumbing had its difficult moments; however, Dink and Bob loved being *old timers*. They treasured living in the mysterious old house and were soon having much more fun at the small, new school than they had had in the large city schools.

Questions for discussion:

1. Who had trouble in the new school?
2. What did Mama do to comfort them?
3. What should we do if we need wisdom?
4. Whose wisdom is better than man's wisdom?
5. To whom does God give wisdom?
6. What would you enjoy doing in this old house?

Graduating class of North Santiam School in 1947.
Roberta was absent the day this photo was taken.

24 Free at Last!

He that covers his sins shall not prosper: but whoever confesses and forsakes them shall have mercy.
Proverbs 28:13

It was evening again. Dink, Bob, Lois and Jimmy were sitting in a circle in the living room listening as Daddy read the horrid story of Achan. (Joshua 7:1-23)

Achan had stolen clothes, gold and silver, and had buried them under his tent. He pretended he had done nothing wrong. What he had done wasn't hidden from God; and in the end, Achan, his family and all he had was burned as punishment for his sins. "Remember your sins will find you," Dad said. "There is nothing hidden from God. The sin you hide today will be there in the morning; and someday, when you are least expecting it, the sin will be discovered. We hope that all sin will be exposed before you die. For if you die with sin in your heart, you will have no other chance to repent and you will be lost forever."

Dink felt heavy. What would happen to her if she died that night? She had stolen like Achan and had kept it hidden for two years. Every day she pretended she was okay, and sometimes she forgot about it. What if she forgot her sin and never repented of it? Just the thought was scary. Also, she was so tired of pretending.

The consistent Christian life of Alvin and Mabel made the presence of God felt in every room of their home. Dink felt God's convicting spirit when she did wrong. She felt His blessings when she behaved correctly. They often said, "Clean your conscience every day." Sometimes they quoted the Bible verse, *Let not the sun go down on your wrath,* (Ephesians 4:26). Because of this, almost every evening someone would apologize for a misbehavior. Dink often apologized for sassing Mama. Sometimes she would ask Lois to forgive her for teasing her until she became angry. Once in a while, Jim would apologize for making Dink angry.

Sometimes even after Dink had apologized and prayed, when she went upstairs into the darkness, she would feel afraid that if she died in the night, she would go to hell. It usually happened on stormy nights, when the tree branches outside her bedroom windows cast ugly shadows over her bed and made clawing noises on the windowpane. She imagined Satan was coming to get her and carry her away from her safe, holy home.

Tonight, the wind growled as it imprisoned the two-story house. The old house squeaked and groaned in protest. The maple tree limbs were clawing at her windows. Dink covered her ears to keep out the screeching and scratching. She drew her arms close to her body so the devil could not snatch one. "Oh, Lord, keep the devil away," she prayed, while Roberta lay snoring beside her.

She stayed awake a long time thinking about the paper money, the stolen candy, the lies she had told to Mama and Daddy. She thought about Tom and Dick and wondered if they remembered the stolen candy. What were they doing in Los Angeles? Were they stealing more candy? Were they going to school as they should? She cried for them because they had no mother. What would she do without a mother? How could she possibly live without the loving words of Mama? Just then, Dink knew she needed her mother. Many times when she could not sleep, she had gone downstairs and knelt beside her mother's bed. Mama would pray for Dink to be forgiven of her sins. After prayer and some tears, Dink would return to the eerie sounds and creepy shadows and go right to sleep.

Dink rolled out of bed and onto the floor. Then crawling around the bed so Roberta would not awake, she tiptoed down the long, dark stairway. The devil sitting on her shoulder, whispered, "You're a fool to be so afraid and run to your mother. Be strong and go back to bed. You'll forget it all by morning." Dink stood on the bottom step, debating whether to go into Mama's room or return to her bed. "Go back to bed," the devil whispered. "Go on back to bed. Don't trouble your mother. She is tired."

Dink turned and started back up the stairs. Then she stopped. "I'm tired of this," she said to herself. Maybe if I pray this time, I'll never be afraid again. She hurried down the few stairs, opened the creaking door and fell on her knees beside her sleeping mother.

"Is that you Dink?" Mabel asked sleepily.

"Yes. I came to pray again."

"You do this every few weeks. Listen, Dink, the Bible says, *If we confess our sins he is faithful and just to forgive us our sins and to cleanse us from all unrighteousness.* (1 John 1:9). Also, Proverbs 28:13 says, *He that covereth his sins shall not prosper but whoever confesses and forsakes them shall have mercy.* I think you are hiding something. You are still guilty after you have prayed; because you are not admitting some wrongs you have done. In a few weeks, you get to feeling so badly again that you come again for prayer. God will forgive and set you free from fear of going to hell when you confess ALL your sins."

A Faithful Father

Dink burst into uncontrollable sobbing. She was shaking like a leaf in a storm. She opened her mouth to confess the stolen candy, but not a squeak came out. She just kept crying.

Daddy was awake now and said, "Get control of yourself and speak up." Alvin controlled himself, and he expected his children to have self-control.

Dink wanted to obey him. She wanted to speak up, but she couldn't find strength to confess something she had denied for two years.

Alvin spoke again.

Dink grunted. That is all she could do.

"Just give her time, Alvin," Mabel said. "Go on back to sleep. You have a hard day of work tomorrow."

Dink waited until she thought Daddy was asleep then she said, "Mama, you remember Mr.—Mr.—that man down at the corner store? Remember when he told Jimmy that I had stolen a sack of candy?"

"Yes."

"Well, I—I—I—did steal it."

"You did? Did you just say that you stole that candy?"

"Yes, I did."

"I'm really surprised you fooled your Daddy. No one fools him."

"I did that time. I never did before nor have I since."

"I can hardly imagine you have carried that guilt for two years. That is why you have been so afraid. Now that you have confessed it, your fear will go away. God will forgive you, and then we'll make things right with Mr. Henry. Tomorrow we will write him a letter and send him the money. Let's pray now."

Dink confessed to God in prayer and the fearful feeling vanished. She was free! She flew up the stairs into the darkness without fear. The storm was still raging outside, the house still groaning, the branches still clawing at the windowpane, and the eerie shadows still sweeping across the room; but Dink lay down unafraid and slept like a baby.

The following day Mama sent money to Mr. Henry. Then Mamma gave Dink plenty of hard work to earn it. She did extra housework for a whole week to pay back one nickel. But she was so happy to be free that she was willing to do it.

Dink was free at last! Now her inside felt like a butterfly that was set free. No more lies. No more pretending. No more feeling afraid.

Questions for discussion:

1. What did the family do each evening?
2. What did Alvin read to his children?
3. Can we hide sin from God?
4. Why was Dink afraid?
5. Why had God not forgiven her when she prayed?
6. Did God forgive after she confessed?

25 Tied in a Cherry Tree

Whatsoever you do, do it heartily, as unto the Lord, and not unto man. Knowing that of the Lord ye shall receive the reward.... Colossians 3:23, 24

A favorite place to play was the apple orchard down the hill behind the house. There were old trees of red Winesap and Johnson apples, "oh, so good." But the apple Dink liked best was a large sweet yellow apple that was as large as a grapefruit. These sometimes grew wild along fencerows. Some called them horse apples. She called them "the best apples in the world."

At times, the old orchard wasn't an apple orchard at all; it became a jungle, a forest, a hide-away, an enormous western ranch. Sometimes they were far away in Africa or South America in a jungle so dense they couldn't see each other. At times, they shrieked as imaginary tigers attacked. Other times, one of them had been trampled by an elephant, and the other one had to help the wounded walk. There were cheetahs and jaguars jumping from tree to tree. The girls would shoot at them.

On some sunny days they played with imaginary monkeys. They fed them pieces of apples or bits of Mama's homemade bread brought from the kitchen. They trained one imaginary monkey to talk. Dink tried very hard to swing from tree to tree as the imaginary monkey did. But she had no tail. Another disadvantage was that since moving to Oregon she had more weight to swing. She was becoming a heavyweight.

In the spring, they ate green apples so juicy and good. Mama constantly cautioned them not to eat too many. But there were many spring nights they rolled in their beds with a stomach complaining about too many green apples. Sometimes those apples came back up in the middle of the night, and they sure didn't taste the same coming up.

They never built a treehouse in the apple orchard. They feared breaking branches would cause them to miss the apples that might have grown on those branches the following spring. Besides, treehouses were for city children, not for those who lived in the wild. It was more fun to balance on the branches, pretending, of course, to be as agile as a monkey.

More often than a jungle, the old apple orchard was the scene of a wildwest battle with Indians. Imaginary Indians lurked behind the bushes that grew where an old apple tree had fallen. From time to time, the Indians shot them with poison arrows, and the wounded limped the remainder of their playtime. Sometimes imaginary warriors hid in the soft hay in the old barn or in the chicken house. The girls would roust them out. While city children of this era learned how to identify real enemy airplanes and how to blackout their homes in case of an enemy attack, their wars in the old apple orchard were with only imaginary enemies. About all that Dink knew of the real war being fought in Europe was that Uncle Aubrey and Cousin Pete were there, and Daddy and Mama prayed every day for their protection. Dink also knew that sugar, butter, tires and many other items could not be bought, because

A Faithful Father

those items were needed in the war. Sometimes she thought the soldiers were faring better than the folks at home.

Dink and Bob could hardly wait for classes to be dismissed in the afternoon so they could play in the apple orchard or the big barn. They were also counting the days when classes would be dismissed for the summer, for then they could pick berries and cherries. These they considered to be *old timers'* jobs, but they seemed like play to the girls.

Dink especially loved cherry picking. She got to climb all day! The cherry orchard owner allowed the smaller children to climb in his trees. There were many cherry orchards in the valley; some were in walking distance from their home. Someone had created a very unique ladder. It was built of wood, with stairs going up from two sides facing each other with a square platform at the top. The stairs were just a little steeper than normal house stairs but easy to climb, and steps were wide enough to stand on for easy picking. Three people could work off this ladder at the same time. Lois and Bob worked on either side of this unique ladder, and Dink on top. Often, Dink would climb out into the tree to pick the cherries in the center of the tree that could not be reached any other way.

One day, they had finished picking all the cherries except those in the center. Bob decided to help Dink pick the remaining cherries. Being afraid of falling, she hunted until she found a rope and tied it securely around her waist. (Thanks to Jim, he had taught her to tie a square knot that would not slip.) Then she climbed up onto the ladder platform and out into the tree. She climbed through the branches to a place where there were many cherries and a large branch on which to stand and another on which to lean. There, she carefully tied the other end of her rope to the branch on which she was leaning and began rapidly filling her bucket. Their buckets were fastened by two hooks onto a large wide belt around the waist. This left both hands free for picking.

Dink was busy picking in another part of the tree and singing, as usual, as loud as possible. Suddenly, she felt the tree shaking violently. She looked around and saw Roberta's legs and arms flying. The next thing she heard was a muffled cry, "Help me, Dink, I'm falling." Roberta was hanging head down, her naked legs treading the air. Her upper body from the waist to head was completely hidden under her long full skirt, while nothing but shorts covered her body from the waist upward to her feet. The rope, secured tightly to the branch where she had been standing, was holding her as she swung like a helpless pendulum in midair.

Dink hurried like a monkey through the branches to the rope and began tugging on it. That only made Bob more uncomfortable by squeezing the rope more tightly at her waist. Then Dink sprang to the ladder and began screaming, "Come! Come! Help! Bob's hung herself in the tree!"

Jimmy and Lois were picking in another tree not far away. Jimmy scampered down his ladder and came running. The rope from which Bob was dangling was squeezing her until she could hardly breathe. Dink hurried back up the tree ahead of Jimmy and tried to cover Roberta's exposed legs by holding a portion of Bob's long full skirt up around her naked legs. Jimmy and Lois moved the heavy platform ladder nearer to Bob. Jim got on it and held up Bob to release the pressure enough that Bob was able to untie the knot that she had so proudly tied. After taking several deep breaths, Bob remarked, "I'll never tie myself in another tree."

Some children would have taken time off to recuperate after such a frightening experience, but not the Hightower children. They had used all their savings, borrowed a pickup, plowed through a blizzard, and endured five freezing days to get to this land of opportunity. The chance to own their own farm in this fertile valley was in sight. Every handful of cherries added a few more pennies to the down payment on that farm.

That evening, while eating, they laughed and talked about Bob's anti-falling-tactics, leaving her hanging upside down in the tree, swinging like a pendulum. When supper was finished, they went out to play. "Catch this ball," Jimmy said, and tossed a football in front of Bob. She ran after the ball and caught it in her arms. Then she tossed it back. Jimmy was playing football in high school and wanted to perfect his skills. Dink swung in the tire swing while they tossed the football, until Daddy called them in for evening worship.

He read the twelfth chapter of Proverbs. "These are wise sayings of King Solomon. He is comparing the rewards of those who live righteous against those who do not," Alvin said. "The eleventh verse reads, *He that tilleth [cultivates] his land shall be satisfied with bread: but he that follows vain persons is void of understanding.* Sometimes it is easier to follow a 'get-rich-quick' idea instead of working hard like we are doing. But here, God's wisdom says a person who follows those vain ideas does not have understanding. He does not realize that he will not be happy even if he does get rich. We have the promise that God will satisfy us if we work. We do not have our own land, but Lord willing we will soon have land if we keep working together like we are doing now," he said, as he gave the children a big smile of approval.

"Verse twenty-four says, *the hand of the diligent* [careful worker] *shall bare rule: but the* slothful [lazy] *shall be under tribute* [heavy taxes to a foreign king]. Being under tribute is working as a slave. We are not slaves. We get paid for our hard work. Why are we working hard?"

"Because we want our own farm," Bob answered.

"Yes, and because you are diligent and working together, God will reward you," Mama told them.

"We sure had to work together today, getting Bob out of the tree," Jimmy added. They all laughed.

"And we trusted God, so we got her untied," Lois added.

"That is right," Mama and Daddy said at the same time.

"I think I also learned a few things today," Bob murmured.

Questions for discussion:

1. Where was a favorite place to play?
2. What happened when they ate many green apples?
3. For what were they working?
4. Were they diligent workers?
5. What is promised to diligent workers?
6. What will happen to those who are lazy?
7. What did Roberta learn?

26 The Day of the Fire

The tongue is a fire, a world of iniquity; so is the tongue among our members, that it defiles the whole body, and sets on fire the course of nature. James 3:6

It was harvest time for green beans. Daddy, Jimmy, Lois, Bob and Dink were picking beans from dawn 'till dark in a field about a half-mile from their home. Mabel carried lunch to them. She spread an oilcloth (a waterproof cloth) onto the ground and put the containers of food, plates, glasses and utensils on it. They sat on their picking buckets around the tablecloth, thanked God for their food and Mabel served each plate in a respectable manner. Meals were a time to relax and reflect on the goodness of God. Alvin usually told stories of his childhood, but not during harvest. Every minute counted. Each one ate quickly and went back to work.

One day, when Mama was serving their lunch, she said, "All morning I've been seeing sparks in the top of that Maple tree in the front yard."

"My, Mabel, is your blood pressure so high that you are seeing sparks?" Alvin asked. Then he laughed.

"Sometimes I do have spots before my eyes," she answered. "But what I saw today were fire sparks, not spots."

Nothing more was said about the sparks. Bob looked over at Dink with a puzzled look on her face. Dink was wondering, are the headaches Mama has so often affecting her mind?

By the time, they got home from work, the wind was calm, so there were no sparks. The following day, there were no beans to pick, so the girls stayed home. Along about noon, the wind began blowing again. Bob and Dink were lying on Jim's bed looking out the north window into the front yard, when the sparks started flying again. They rushed down the long stairway and into the kitchen, "Mama! There is fire in the tree again, like you saw yesterday. See, the new little branches are hitting the electric line when the wind blows," Dink shouted, as she was pulling Mabel toward the open door. "What if the tree catches on fire?"

"Shall we run and get Daddy?" Bob asked.

"Yes," she answered. Then paused. "No, I believe I better go so I can convince him of the urgency," she said. "You girls stay out of the front yard. And Dink, don't try climbing that tree and pulling the little branches away from the wire. You'll get yourself killed. There is tremendous power in those wires. I'll be right back," she said; then she rushed down the graveled road toward the bean field.

Dink looked up at the wire and wondered how there could be dangerous power in a wire. She worked around wires almost every day. Two wires were strung down each row in both the berry and bean fields. One wire on the bottom of the row, another on the top. The bean vines grew on strings woven between these two wires. That made harvesting easier. "We touch wires every day while we are picking or when we hoe weeds from around the plants," she said to Bob. "How can power be in a wire? And what kind of power? It sounds so strange."

A Faithful Father

"Oh, forget it," Bob said. "Let's go watch from the window." They dashed back upstairs and lay on Jim's bed again. "This is like firecrackers on the Fourth of July," Bob said. They laughed and talked about firecrackers for a while; and then suddenly, blazes about three feet high shot up! Dink covered her head with a pillow.

Lois was standing at the east window watching the road for Daddy to come and take charge of the dangerous situation. Soon she called, "I see Daddy and Jim running."

Before Alvin and Jimmy got to the house, the whole treetop burst into flames. Then, right before their eyes, one wire melted into two pieces. One fell into the tall dry grass alongside the road where they were running. Instantly, the grass in front of their house ignited into six-foot flames. The flames almost hid Daddy and Jimmy. Lois screamed. It was the latter part of July. The tall dry grass hadn't seen water for six weeks or maybe longer.

The girls rushed downstairs and outside. The high voltage wire lay hidden in the flames. When Daddy saw Bob and Dink rushing out the door, he yelled, "Stay back! It's instant death for whoever touches that *live-wire!* Hurry, pump a tub full of water. And Jim, run to the henhouse and bring all the gunny sacks you can find. This fire could destroy the whole country."

Bob and Dink dashed around the house. Lois went walking through the house and picked up a tub. They got to the water pump just as Lois placed the round galvanized tub under the pump. Bob pumped as fast as she could until she was exhausted. Then Lois took the handle and pumped until she was tired. By now, Daddy and Jimmy had come to carry the tub of water nearer to the flames. Lois put another tub under the pump spout, while Bob and Dink dashed to the front yard.

"The other wire has fallen and is lying on the gravel in the road. You girls stay in the backyard away from the fire and the road, and keep pumping water," Daddy demanded, as he and Jim set the tub of water down in the front yard. Dad plunged the dry gunny sacks into the tub and kneaded the water into the sacks until they were saturated. Then he and Jim ran and began beating the burning grass nearest to the house.

The flames were getting closer and closer to the house that contained everything the family owned. The house was old and the lumber as dry as the summer grass that was rapidly dissolving into ashes.

"Oh, Lord, save our house and all we own," Dink heard Mabel praying. She had just returned from the store, where she had called the fire department and the electric company.

From the sideyard, Dink hollered, "Can I come and help?"

"Just keep pumping water," Dad shouted above the roar of the flames. Roberta and Dink ran to the pump and began pumping another tub of water.

While they pumped, Dink, asked Bob, "Why do people call me a 'live wire'?"

"I suppose it's because you can't be still," she answered.

"But Daddy said that the wire was alive. It's not wiggling. And Mama said it was powerfully dangerous. How can a wire be dangerous or alive? It looks plumb dead to me."

Lois interrupted the conversation, as she often did, saying. "When you grow up, you will study about electricity, and then you will understand."

Dink put her hands on her hips and retorted. "I'm grown up now, so why can't I know now?"

"This ain't no time to be fussin'," Bob scolded. "We need to be being really good so God will keep our house from burnin' down."

By now, neighbors had come to help beat out the flames. The girls had to keep pumping to have water to rewet the sacks each time one dried out. "Beating the flames with wet sacks is the only defense we have against this wildfire," one neighbor said. "The nearest fire department is miles away in Jefferson, and the electric company is about 20 miles away. This whole country would be burned to ashes if we waited on them."

The flames were traveling in all directions. Fortunately, Mr. James, the owner of the property, had recently mowed around the house and the pasture that was between the apple orchard and the house. The grass was shorter and the fire easier to put out. After Alvin, Jimmy and the men had the flames under control, Daddy allowed the girls to get wet gunny sacks and to beat out any smoke or flames they saw.

When the electric serviceman finally arrived, the burning grass was almost completely out. However, they watched it carefully until after dark, stamping out any flames that flared up. The tree was still smoking. The men climbed into the tree and cut about half of it off. They also repaired the line that had burned.

When the family gathered for worship that evening, they talked about how fast the fire burned, how dangerously close it was to destroying all they owned, and how thankful they were that the fire was out and their home was still standing. Then, using the little sparks as examples, Daddy talked about how small beginnings sometimes end up causing terrible trouble.

He told a story about a dike that had just a tiny hole near the bottom. As the water rushed through the little hole, the hole grew and grew and grew until the sea flooded the homes in the low land. The people had to run to keep from being drowned. He opened his Bible and read James 3:3-6: *We put bits in the horses' mouths... and we turn about their whole body. Behold the ships also which though they be so great... are turned about with a very small helm. Even so the tongue is a little member, and boasts great things! Behold, how great a matter a little fire kindles. The tongue is a fire, a world of iniquity....* He laid down the Bible and said, "Sometimes a little gossip can start a rumor that can spread like a wildfire, hurting many along the way. It could cause jealousy and someone to get killed," he said.

"Also, watch little evil thoughts or attitudes in your life," Mabel added, "for they can develop into habits that you may not be able to control. Anger, dishonesty, or envy may start from tiny thoughts, but they may grow until they cause lots of trouble."

Each one prayed as usual. However, their prayers were more than words, because they came from thankful hearts. They were praising God for protecting them. They were also asking God to help them destroy little habits before they became big problems.

Questions for discussion:

1. What did Mama see in the tree?
2. What developed from those tiny sparks?
3. Did the family work together?
4. How did they get the fire out?
5. What are some little things that can cause big problems?
6. What should we do with bad attitudes?

27 Silly Raccoons

Likewise, ye younger, submit yourselves unto the elder. Yea, all of you be subject one to another, and be clothed with humility: for God resists the proud, and gives grace to the humble. 1 Peter 5:5

Dink was sitting up on the roof of the east porch, when she saw Daddy walking on the gravel road coming home from work. King, their Collie/German shepherd mix dog, ran to meet him. Dink climbed quickly back inside Jimmy's bedroom, hoping that Daddy hadn't seen her on the roof again. She ran downstairs shouting to Bob. "Daddy's coming home and he is carrying something. It must be an animal 'cause King keeps jumping up trying to smell it."

The girls ran to meet him. "What you got?" Dink called. Alvin stopped and opened the little box he was carrying.

"Baby raccoons," he said, "and they've had nothing to eat today. Mr. Miles shot their mother this morning."

"Why'd he do that?" Dink stormed, with her hands on her hips.

"Because she had been sneaking into his chicken house and eating his eggs."

"Will they bite?" Bob asked, as she extended her hand to pet them. The baby coons only looked at her and wrinkled up their noses, as if smelling her hand.

"Let's try to get them some warm milk to drink," Daddy said. He sat down on the back-porch steps with the box of baby raccoons.

"We need to warm some milk to give the baby coons Daddy brought home," Bob said, as she dashed into the kitchen where Mama was cooking supper.

"Baby raccoons?" Mama questioned. "We can hardly keep the twin goats fed enough to keep them alive."

"This place is becoming like a zoo," Lois said, "with chickens, rabbits, a pig, twin baby goats, cats, King and now raccoons." She went out and peeked into the box. "Oh, they are so cute. We can feed them with our doll bottles."

Bob brought a doll bottle and let the warm milk drip onto the baby coon's nose. "He likes it," Dink squealed. "Look! He's licking it off."

"You will need to feed them often," Alvin said, "just like a mother does a newborn baby. Every time you give the baby goats a bottle of milk, give some to the coons, too."

In a few weeks, the raccoons were large enough to suck a baby bottle nipple. As soon as school was dismissed each day, Dink and Bob ran home to feed the coons. The coons lay in the girls' arms on their backs just like a human baby. In this prone position, the coons soon learned to hold their bottles with their tiny little front paws. When the bottle was low in milk, they learned to push up the end of the bottle with their back paws until the last drop of milk oozed out.

The poor twin goats might have been jealous. Who knows, for the coons got most of the attention. However, Alvin didn't allow the other animals to be neglected.

One time before the coons learned about fire, the family was sitting around the table eating supper, when they smelled hair burning. Jimmy jumped up, and following the smell, he found one of the raccoons backing into the fireplace. The hair on her tail was smoking. Fur on her back stood straight up, and she was hissing like an angry cat. She bit and clawed at Jimmy when he tried to get her away from the fire. Dink tried and Bob did, too. Finally, in desperation, Daddy grabbed the broom and swept the raccoon to the other side of the room. Then Jimmy slapped a heavy towel over the animal and held her tail in the bucket of cold water which had been left after mopping the kitchen. After the animal calmed down, Lois cut off the burned hair and wrapped its tail in a cold, wet cloth.

Both raccoons loved eggs. One time, Alvin came late to the table and found the raccoon holding his soft cooked egg carefully on the palm of her little paw while she was sucking up the liquid yolk. Alvin stood very still and watched while the raccoon ate the entire soft poached egg without spilling one drop.

They also loved jelly. Mabel stored some of her homemade jelly in odd jars that had no lids. She sealed the jars by pouring melted paraffin (wax) over the jelly. These jars of jelly were stored on the high shelves of the pantry. Grandma Lou Hightower had come that summer to help with the housework, so Mabel could care for the garden and work with the children in the fields. One afternoon when she awoke from a nap, she heard noises coming from the pantry. Grandma had come from Los Angeles, California, where she always had a phone and plenty of people to call when she needed help. Who could she call today? There was no phone, and the family was working several miles away on another man's farm.

Grandma peeked quietly through a crack in the pantry door. She saw red strawberry jelly splattered on the pantry wall and on the legs of the worktable. On the floor lay the broken jar. A broken jar of blackberry jelly lay on the bottom shelf. One coon was happily licking the blackberry jelly around jagged pieces of glass. The other coon was sitting on the top shelf, holding a jar of jelly with one paw and spooning handsful of jelly into his mouth using the other paw.

She jerked the door open quickly! Then waving her hands wildly, she yelled loudly, "Get out of here." The coons glared at her, but they did not move. She had seen the children handling the coons like kittens, so she reached for the one on the bottom shelf. The coon dug its claws into her arm, leaving strips of open flesh for six inches down her arm and then bit into her hand near the thumb. She knocked the coon loose and it ran. With a broom, she shooed the one off the top shelf.

A family council was held that night. Despair was thick enough to slice. Grandma, whom they highly respected and their only grandparent, was badly wounded. Would the pets have to go? Grandma insisted we must rid our home of wild beasts. After much deliberation, it was decided we would keep the animals in their cages when we were away. The first time they were forgotten and left out, they would have to go. While Grandma was there, the children never once forgot to lock them up.

Their raccoons were both females. After Grandma had gone back to Los Angeles, Dad traded one of their coons for a male from the man who raised the other two coons from the same litter. His were both males. After the male came to live with the Hightowers, their female took up his habits of wandering away from the yard, growling at anyone who came near her food, and several other bad habits. Often in the evening, they would have to go into the apple orchard behind the house or the grove of trees across the road to search for the coons before caging them up for the night. One time they stayed out all night. From then on, the male was kept in his cage, but the female could be out when the children were home.

About a month later, when the girls came home from school, one of the twin goats was missing. They looked in the orchard, in the barn, in the grove across the road. At this time, they had a party line telephone, so they called all the neighbors who had telephones. No one had seen the pet goat.

It was getting toward evening. They stopped looking for the goat so they could do the chores, chop and carry in wood, gather eggs, feed and water the chickens, rabbits, pigs and the coons. When Bob went to give food and water to the coons, the male coon was missing! She ran to tell Mama. "So, the male coon is missing?" Bob shook her head. "That coon is probably somewhere eating the goat," Mama said. "Why don't you crawl under the house and look?"

"Oh, no," Bob said, "that coon will bite me."

The girls had to carry in the wood, while Jimmy crawled under the house looking for the coon. He found the goat, dead. Jimmy took a pitch fork and drug the goat out. The coon was growling loudly and hanging onto the goat with all his might.

Soon, another council was held about the fate of the coons. "I don't think your coons are happy," Dad said. "Their animal instincts are calling them to live in the wild. What do you say, shall we let them go?"

"But they don't know how to hunt for their food," Mabel protested.

"They will starve to death," Dink wailed.

"Or some coyote will eat them for his dinner," Roberta complained.

"But we can't keep them much longer; winter is coming and they can't get enough exercise in their cage to keep them warm. They will freeze."

"Don't they sleep all winter?" Dink asked. "We could make a warm nest in a corner of the wood shed."

"No, they don't sleep all winter," Jimmy added, as if disgusted that Dink didn't know.

"Mr. Trimble wants to buy them," Dad said. "He has a motel in Newport Beach, and he keeps a few animals to interest the people."

"Will he take good care of them?" Bob asked.

"I'm sure he will," Dad said. "He's a good man. He is Sis. Ruby Stover's brother."

After a long discussion, they decided to sell their pets to Mr. Trimble.

Lois, Bob and Dink cried as Mr. Trimble was driving away with their babies. However, they knew it would be best for the raccoons to have someone caring for them, because they had not learned to hunt for food nor to avoid predators. The girls were also happy because they had submitted to their parents' authority.

Questions for discussion:

1. Why were the baby raccoons without a mother?
2. Why did Mr. Miles shoot the mother?
3. What is the eighth commandment?
4. Did stealing cause problems for the raccoons?
5. Will stealing cause problems for people?
6. Were the girls happy because they submitted to their parents?

28 Caught on The Train Bridge

At the times of this ignorance God winked at; but now commands men everywhere to repent.
Acts 17:30

"I sure wish Daddy would hurry up and come for us," Dink complained. "I'm so tired of picking berries. He said he'd be here by five o'clock."

"Yeah, it's late, but he'll be here soon," Roberta said. "In fact, I see him coming now." She pointed to his pickup coming down the lane to Mr. Bethel's berry patch.

Alvin stopped his pickup at the end of the rows of boysenberries. "Say girls, I want to visit a little with Brother Bethel if he isn't busy," he said, from the open window of the pickup. "I'm going to his house to see. If I don't come back really soon, you'll know I'm going to be talking with him for a while."

"Okay, we'll wait." Lois told him. "Can we quit picking?"

"Yes. Put your berries all in the same crate and I'll tell him how many you have picked today." Bob and Dink handed Lois the boxes they had filled with berries, and she put them into a new crate. "Looks like you did really good today. You have earned a lot of money today to help buy our own farm. Now, mark your row where you stopped picking, so you don't waste time in the morning picking over what you have already picked today," he said. "Then rest until I come back." He drove back to Bethel's house which was at the front part of the farm.

The girls were tired, so they just sat down in the shade. When Daddy didn't come back soon, they knew he would be talking a long, long time. He and Bro. Bethel always talked a long time, discussing Bible doctrines such as, what is adultery? when was the Church founded? or questions about the second coming of Christ. Dink was wondering what they would be discussing today.

Bob was drawing pictures in the sand, when Dink said, "Bob, we've been wanting to see what's on the other side of the river. Wouldn't this be a good time to go see?"

"I think so. We usually have to leave as soon as we have finished working. Let's go." They both jumped to their feet and started toward the bridge.

"Don't go; it's about time for the six o'clock train," Lois warned.

"You are just trying to scare us," Dink retorted.

"It really is almost time for the train. Remember, Jimmy and Bill almost got killed by that six o'clock train"

"But they tried to beat the train. We'll come back if we hear it nearing," Dink called back.

"Isn't it strange how good we feel when there is a chance to do something we want to do?" Bob said, as they were running.

The bridge was high near the berry patch and much higher at the riverbank. The girls ran a long distance back toward Bethel's house to a place where the train bridge was low enough to get on. Once on, they bravely stretched their legs across the cracks between the railroad ties. Lois ran along on the ground beside them warning them with every breath.

They ignored her warning; but when they finally got out over the river, Dink said, "Wow! It looks scary! What if we should fall? We can't swim."

"We can't fall through these eight-inch cracks," Bob remarked; "they are too small, and the protective framework is high on either side."

"What if the train comes when you girls are in the middle of the river?" Lois called for the last time to her little sisters.

Dink looked at Roberta. The question, "What if?" was in both their eyes.

"We'll beat it and stay on the other side until it passes," Dink called down to Lois, as she and Bob hurried out over deeper water.

The North Santiam River was very deep and wide. The warm spring weather had melted much snow in the mountains. All that extra water was flowing into the river, making it deeper and wider than usual. The water was also ice cold. Even good swimmers sometimes drown because the cold temperature of the water causes their muscles to cramp. The farther out the girls went, the more Dink realized what a trap they would be in if the train did come; so she hurried faster and faster. Bob could hardly keep up with her. Within a short time, they were about halfway across the wide river.

Dink looked down at the deep-rushing water. It whirled in turbulence, as if racing against the flood of incoming melting snow. "It seems more-scary out here," she remarked.

Bob, too frightened to talk, whispered, "Yeah it is scary, and Dink, I think I hear the train whistling."

"You're just afraid," Dink said and started running faster.

"No, I'm not. Stop! Stop and listen carefully," Bob pleaded.

Dink was already scared, so she stopped. Sure enough, in the distance, she could hear the faint whine of the train whistle. "Which side are we closest to?" she asked.

"We're in the middle," Bob wailed. "But I think we better go back. If we can get past the water, we might jump. Hurry, Dink, hurry," and she wheeled around and began running back the way they had just come.

Dink scampered behind her.

> (Let me explain how hard it is to run on a train bridge. You may have seen railroad ties in stores that sell garden supplies. They are big, twelve-inch square black boards about five feet long. The bridge was constructed of railroad ties set about eight inches apart. Since a tie is twelve inches square, to run a person has to leap over a twelve-inch tie and two eight-inch spaces at every other step. The next leap is over two twelve-inch ties and one eight-inch space. If a runner missed landing on the tie, he would trip. To step on each tie, he might trip over his own feet and fall. If a tie is missed and the foot falls into the open space the runner would fall, probably would break a leg and the strong metal train would crush him to death.)

Both girls knew their life depended on the accuracy of landing on every third board. Dink's heart was racing, her face flushed, and her soul was praying for God's protection and forgiveness for not listening to Lois.

Each time the whistle blew, it was louder and louder and louder! They dared not run faster for fear of mis-stepping and falling. Running had to be rhythmically perfect, or they were dead. *What if Bob fell and I couldn't get her to the end of the bridge?* Dink questioned. *What if I fell? I know she would not leave me alone. She has always protected me. We would both be pulverized by*

A Faithful Father

the heavy train while trying to help each other. But Dink could not let her mind wander. She must concentrate on running, running, running, one step short, next step long, one step short, next step long, in perfect rhythm.

The bridge was shaking violently, so they knew the train was near. Dink glanced back but still didn't see it, however, the vibration was constantly getting stronger. They knew it was on the far end of the bridge, hidden only by the curve and the tall trees. "Oh Lord, help us," Dink prayed, and then she shouted, "Hurry Bob!"

"Hush," Bob called back. "You'll make me fall." Dink knew that was true. Bob had to stay perfectly focused on where each foot was landing.

Dink repeated to herself, "Don't fall, the train will grind you into *people burger*. Don't fall– Don't fall!"

They cleared the water, but the bridge was far too high to jump to the ground. Lois had waited at the river bank for her foolish little sisters. She was shouting, "Jump! The sand is soft. Jump! Jump!"

"We can't," they both shouted and kept running. By now, a sharp pain was stabbing into Dink's side. She slowed down and looked back. The train was right behind her! She could feel heat from the engine. For a second, strength left her legs. Dink looked at Roberta. She was as pale as a sheet of white paper. Dink felt sorry for Bob; she knew she had gotten Bob into this mess.

"Jump off! Jump off!" Lois was yelling, as she ran along beside the high bridge.

"I'm coming," Bob shouted and away she went.

The timbers that held the bridge were rough and full of splinters. "Climb down and slide down a post," she shouted up to Dink.

Dink scooted off the bridge and locked her legs around the post, but she clung to a tie overhead with her hands. She was too afraid to jump as Bob did. She gripped the tie above her head with all her might as the train came roaring over them. The shrill whistle blasted their ears.

"Turn loose and fall," Bob shouted above the roar of the engine.

"It's too far to the ground," Dink cried.

The bridge was swinging. Dink closed her eyes and clung desperately. Would the bridge break? Would the train mash her hands? Was she going to die after running so far?

"You won't get hurt on the ground!" Bob yelled again. "Let go!" Lois too was shouting, "Let go! The sand is soft!"

The engine had passed, but the cars were still roaring over Dink's head. She still couldn't turn loose. Finally, while the train caboose was passing over her, she let go. At last she was safe on the solid earth again. She covered her ears with her hands until the noisy, horrid train had gone a good distance away, then she breathed deeply.

"I'm gonna tell Daddy," Lois said angrily.

"Oh, please don't. Daddy will spank us. You don't like spankings, so why get us a spanking?" Dink cried.

"Yeah, Lois, we already got our punishment. We've learned our lesson," Bob said.

"You were tempting God; that is what you were doing, and the Bible says, 'Thou shall not tempt the Lord thy God.' You both need to repent."

"Okay, okay we will, just don't tell Daddy," Dink pleaded. "I'll wash dishes in your place tonight if you won't tell."

"We do a lot of things for you," Bob argued, "now you do us a favor."

Lois finally promised she would not tell. Then Bob and Dink lay down in the sand to get cooled off and quit breathing so hard.

A Faithful Father

"We must not let Daddy hear us breathing hard. He will question us about what we have been doing. And if we told a lie, we'd have to repent of that too," Bob said.

That night, Dink prayed first; "Thank you Jesus for bringing us home safe. Thank you Jesus that you watched over us and protected us today. Bless Mama and Daddy, Jimmy, Lois, Bob and me and do, Jesus, bless everybody. In Jesus name."

As soon as they got up from prayer, Jimmy asked, "What did you do today that made you want to pray first? You are usually the last one to pray." Then turning to Mama, he said, "Mom, you better find out what Dink has been doing today?"

"Yes, I'll take care of her. You take care of Jimmy," Mabel answered.

Bob and Dink looked at Lois with a threatening look and said, "Come on Lois, let's get to bed." And quickly they ran upstairs.

"I wonder why those girls are so anxious to get into bed tonight?" Alvin asked.

Questions for discussion:

1. What did Roberta and Dink want to do?
2. Why did Lois warn them?
3. Where were Dink and Bob when the train whistled?
4. Did Lois think they should repent for tempting God?
5. Did Lois show compassion for her sisters?
6. Should they have followed Lois' advice?
7. Did Dink appreciate God's protection?

29 A Ben Franklin Kite

And be not conformed to this world: but be ye transformed by the renewing of your mind, that ye may prove what [is] that good, and acceptable, and perfect, will of God. Romans 12:2

Bob was pushing Dink on the tire swing that hung from another big maple tree that grew in the back yard. Jimmy was sitting on the porch steps watching the girls. "Let's make a kite today. We don't have to work and the wind is blowing just right to fly a kite!"

Jumping off the swing, Dink said, "I'll make the paste and get some newspapers."

"I'll find some string," Bob added.

"I have some sticks I've been saving in the woodshed," Jimmy said, and he hurried down the steps heading for the woodshed. He brought back two straight sticks. One was about three feet long and another, a little shorter, maybe twenty inches long. He sat down on the porch steps and began whittling off the bark and knots.

A Faithful Father

Dink found the newspapers on the floor beside Daddy's chair. In a small bowl, she mixed water into white flour until it was the consistency of paste. These she took to Jim on the porch. After the sticks were clean, Jimmy cut tiny notches into the end of each stick and tied the two sticks together to form a cross. Then he strung kite string, that Bob had found, through these slits to form a frame the shape of a diamond. He laid the sticks on the newspaper and cut the paper two inches larger than the string frame.

Dink wiped the paste she had made over about two inches of the outside edges of the newspaper. Now, Jimmy carefully folded the paper over the string frame, pressing it down tightly.

While Jim was gluing on the paper, Dink cut four two-inch squares of paper, which Jim glued on the top and bottom tips for reinforcement. While this was drying, they tore rags and tied them together to form a tail to balance the kite. "Did you know that Ben Franklin made a kite like this one and used it to prove that lightning had electricity in it?" Jim asked.

"Really?" Dink asked.

"Yeah, he tied a key to his kite and flew it in a storm. The lightning sparked on the metal key."

"Did it travel down the string and shock him?"

"I don't know," Jim answered. "Now let's get the string and tail tied on. First, we have to tie string to the top and bottom of the kite and to both sides then connect our long ball of string to the center of it where these strings and the two sticks are crossed." When that was finished, he tied the tail to the longest point of the frame. "Now the kite is ready to fly," he said, holding it high over his head. "But we had better let it dry in the sun a little longer."

"That is just as good as the kites we buy at the store," Dink remarked.

"It's much better," Jim answered. "It's stronger, cause these sticks are stronger and our tail is longer. It will fly longer and higher than those store-bought kites."

"Do you think Ben Franklin made his kite?"

"Sure, he did. There were no kites in stores that long ago," Jimmy answered.

"Hey, why don't we make a box kite while that one is drying?" Bob suggested. "Don't you have some little narrow boards?"

"I don't have enough," Jim answered.

"Maybe Mama will let us go down to Mr. James' store and buy some," Dink suggested.

So while the Ben Franklin Kite was drying, they built a box kite. It consisted of four rectangular shape frames glued together and paper pasted on all four sides. Both ends were open. While the box kite was drying, they flew the other kite.

That evening, when they gathered around the table for supper, Alvin asked, "What did you children do today?"

"We made a Ben Franklin kite," Dink answered quickly.

"Why did you call it a Ben Franklin kite?"

"'Cause Jimmy said it was like the one he hung a key on to find electricity," Dink answered.

Alvin laughed and asked, "Did yours fly like Ben Franklin's?"

"Of course," Jim answered, "after we got the tail the right length. At first, the tail was too long."

Turning to Lois, he asked, "What did you do?"

"I helped Mama; she is making Bob and Dink twin dresses out of some pretty flour sacks."

"Wanna see it?" Bob asked, and she ran into the kitchen to get the material off the sewing machine.

"Oh, it's so pretty!" Dink said, clapping her hands.

"Yes, it is very pretty," Alvin agreed. Then turning to Jimmy, he asked, "So, the tail of your kite was too heavy?"

"Yes," Jim answered.

"The tail gives the kite balance. Just as the kite needs balance so it can fly high, our lives need balance so we can fly high in the Lord. God is balanced. He is balanced between love and justice. Some people think God is a strong, mean power that is ready to destroy anyone who doesn't please him. Others believe God is only love, and that He does not chastise humans for disobeying His commandments."

Mabel spoke up, "Maybe the children don't understand a balance."

"I know what balance is," Dink said. "It's when you can stand on a teeter-totter and both ends of the teeter-totter are the same height from the ground."

"That is correct. The teeter-totter is balanced. Here is another illustration of balance: Years ago, people used a balance scale to weigh things for sale. If I asked for five pounds of sausage, the clerk would place a five-pound weight on one side of the scales. On the other side of the scales, he would place a scoop of meat on a wax paper. If the meat side of the balance was higher than the weight side, more meat was added until the two sides were even. If the scoop of meat was lower than the five-pound weight, some sausage would be taken off until the two sides were equal. When the two sides were even, the scales were balanced, just as the teeter-tooter was balanced."

Daddy had been hunting through his Bible. When Mabel finished talking, he read Hebrews 12:28-29, . . . *let us have grace, whereby we may serve God acceptably with reverence and godly fear: For our God is a consuming fire.* You see children, we must be serious about what we do and say, so that all we do is acceptable to God. But we must not fear that God is hard to please, because 1 John 4:7 says, *Beloved let us love one another, for God is love...*

"What God's word says is on one side of the balance. What we do and say is on the other side. God said, 'Honor your father and your mother.' If you honor your father and mother, your life is in balance because it is equal to God's commandment."

"That's easy to understand," Jimmy said. "Just like four plus six equals the same as five plus five, both sides of the equation are equal. The equation is balanced."

"What the Bible says and what we do have to agree?" Lois asked, "like the two sides of that equation, each equal ten?"

"That is correct," Daddy answered.

"The Bible says, *Let not the sun go down on your wrath.* So if we are angry at someone and we apologize before we go to bed, we are in balance?" Lois asked.

"Exactly," Daddy answered. "One side of the scales has God's instruction, *don't let the sun go down on your wrath.* When we obey, obedience is on the other side. The scale is then balanced.

"Here is another thought about being in balance so we can have a successful walk with Christ," Alvin continued. "Our time should also be balanced. Some of our time is for studying God's Word and for praying, some for work and play. The Bible says, *he that does not work shall not eat,* and each one must eat so each one must work."

"So it's okay to play and to work, but if we work and play all day and have no time for Jesus, we are out of balance?" Bob asked.

"Yes," Daddy answered. "Neither should we just read the Bible and pray and not work. I knew a woman who thought that she should only read and pray. Her husband was old and not well, but she would not help him because she was doing God's work, so she said. She was not balanced. Helping her sick husband was also her work for God." He paused waiting for other comments.

Mabel spoke, "Now do you understand how balance is important in our lives as well as in flying a kite?" They nodded, yes.

A Faithful Father

For worship that night they sang number 395, in *Evening Light Songs*.

> "Weighed in the Balance"
> Weighed by the Word which is given now,
> Search it and know thou art pure.
> Unto it's mandates [commands] in meekness bow,
> Then thou shalt be secure.
>
> There it will hurt like a wounding dart
> When that dread answer will fall.
> Weighed and found wanting will pierce thy heart,
> At the last judgement call.
>
> CHORUS
> //Weighed and found wanting//
> Rejected at Heaven's door.
> —B.E. Warren

The children felt really serious after singing that song, so they asked God to forgive them for even minor offences. Then they apologized to each other and ran happily up the stairs to their beds.

Questions for discussion:

1. What was needed so the kite would fly?
2. What is needed for us to fly to heaven?
3. With what do we balance ourselves?
4. How can we balance with God's Word?
5. Who is the judge that will decide if we are balanced?

30 A Lonesome Winter

See that you do not despise one of these little ones, for I say to you that their angels in heaven continually see the face of My Father who is in heaven.
Matthew 18:10 paraphrased

"You look so tired," Mabel said to Alvin when he sat down to eat supper. "You are also limping more than usual. Is your leg hurting again?" Alvin nodded. "You need to stop working so hard."

"But I love to work," he protested. "I have always loved physical activity. When I was a youngster, I could outrun all my friends and could jump as high as my height."

"Oh, Daddy, you couldn't do that," Jimmy said.

"Oh, yes, I could. I was light-footed like a deer. But let's thank God for our food and then we can talk." Each one bowed his head while Daddy prayed, and then he continued talking. "My friends could hold a stick over my head. I would back up a little distance and then jump right over it without knocking the stick off their hands. I did it many times."

"Wow! That really was hard to do!" Dink said.

"Did you use a pole-vaulting stick?" Jimmy asked.

"No, I used nothing," Alvin answered. "I just jumped. When I was a child, the whole community had picnics and fish fries together. The boys would play games and compete with each other running, jumping, wrestling and racing our horses. I could outrun most everyone near my age, until I broke my leg."

"Tell us again how you broke it?" Bob asked.

Alvin leaned over and rubbed his leg. "A team of horses got spooked when a jackrabbit jumped out in front of them. They took off running really fast, dragging the plow behind them. To get them stopped, I pulled with all my might on only one side. I knew that if I would get them going in a circle, they would stop. The plow caught my leg as it was spinning around. It twisted my leg, causing it to break in several places.

"My dad carried me on his horse to the doctor's house. My leg was mangled so badly the doctor thought it best to cut it off, but my dad told the doctor, 'A bad leg is better than no leg at all.' And he would not sign the paper giving the doctor permission to amputate my leg. So, you can thank your Grandpa Hightower that I have two legs today."

"Were you very old when that happened?" Lois asked.

"I was fourteen. Methods for treating broken bones were different in those days. Heavy boards were strapped on both sides of my leg to hold the broken pieces together. Those boards were so heavy that I could not move. When I tried to move, the pain was unbearable. I lay in bed for four weeks without turning over. Weeks later, when I was able to be up and walking with crutches, I fell and broke the same leg again.

"Then I had to lie in one position for another three weeks. Children, be careful and don't break your bones. Always be thankful for your good legs. I've had to limp all my life since that time, because one of my legs is a little shorter than the other one.

"My crippled leg aches most of the time, especially in rainy weather like we are having now. And it is very hard for me to work in this rain; besides, there isn't much work in the country during the winter. I haven't told you children, but Uncle Cornelius said he could get me a job where he is working in California. I'm thinking of going to Los Angeles to work. They say it rains all winter here in Oregon. If I work during this winter, all the money we have earned could be saved to buy a farm."

"You'll be gone all winter?" Bob questioned. "And be gone at Christmas?"

"I'll try to come home for Christmas," he promised.

Mabel washed and ironed Daddy's clothes and packed them in a cardboard box. He tied the box with a rope and left on the Greyhound bus.

Alvin sent letters home with money orders for Mabel to buy what the family needed. Mama couldn't drive and Jimmy was too young to have a license. When she needed something that Mr. James did not have in his little country store, he would get it for her when he went to Salem to buy groceries to restock his store shelves. Mabel only needed a few things from the store, because she had preserved berries, peaches, apples, quinces, corn, beans, peas, carrots, peppers, tomatoes, squash and meats during the summer.

Mama read Daddy's letters during family worship time. Sometimes she cried while reading them. It was the first time that Mabel had been without the comfort and security she found in Alvin those many years ago after her papa had died. Bob and Lois usually cried too, but Dink thought crying made her look like a baby, so she would wait until she went to bed. Then she would cry herself to sleep. Bob would hug her.

In one letter, Alvin asked if it was still raining. Mama took down the calendar from the kitchen wall and counted the days she had marked since she last saw the sun. She counted through part of October and all of November. She wrote back to Alvin: "It's been forty-nine days since we have seen the sun. It came out a few hours today."

The days and nights seemed so long when Daddy wasn't there. All day every day, Dink missed her Daddy. As she ran home from school, she hoped that Daddy would be waiting for her in his chair. At night, when the wind blew ghostly and the rain continuously pattered on the roof, she felt heavy and achy. She missed her Daddy's soft voice reading the Bible and praying before she went to bed. When he was home, his voice resounding in her head made her feel secure as she climbed the stairs to her bedroom. Every evening, when Mama called the children to family worship, Dink would ask, "When will Daddy come home?"

"Look at King, he is missing Daddy, too," Bob added. "He is a sad dog. He whines and groans when he sleeps beside Daddy's chair."

In the long evenings, Mama played games with the children and read many stories. She busied herself sewing and showing Lois and Bob how to embroidery and crochet. She sang comforting songs, but just the same, the days and evenings were long and gloomy.

When December came and snow hung on the fir trees, it reminded them of Christmas. "Will Daddy be here for Christmas?" one or another of the children would ask almost daily.

"We hope so," Mabel would always answer.

One lonely night, just before Christmas, someone knocked on the back door while they were singing. Bob was sitting nearest to the door, so Mama told her to see who it was. She was a little frightened, because most respectable people knocked at the front door. Could it be a bum seeking food? A robber? King was also frightened. He jumped up, his hair stood high on his back, his tail arched and he was growling. He darted for the door ahead of Bob. She hesitated at the door, fearful to open it. Suddenly, King began wagging his tail and scratching at the door. When Bob saw King's actions, she thought someone King knew was there, so she opened the door. "Daddy!" she squealed and fell into his open arms.

Instantly, the whole family dropped their song books and ran to the door. Everyone was trying to hug Daddy at once, until he almost fell off the back porch. "Let me get in. It's cold out here," he said. "Then we can all hug."

Daddy came with many boxes. Bro. Bethel, who had picked him up in Jefferson, helped him carry them into the house. After they were through hugging, Daddy said, "The boxes on the table have Christmas fruit— oranges, apples, and grapefruit. You children have gifts in that box," he said and pointed to a box Bro. Bethel had just set down. You may open them tomorrow morning."

"And what did you bring for Mama?" Lois asked. "Where is her gift?"

"Mabel loves food," Alvin said teasing, "She can have the largest portion of all the fruit."

"No," Dink said stomping her foot, "Mommy needs a present, too."

"I will take Mama to town so she can pick out her very special gift. Is that all right, little Miss Livewire? And have you gotten a little out of hand while I was away? Looks like I may have to straighten you out again."

Dink hung her head.

Then Daddy asked, "Have you all been working together while I was away?"

Mabel spoke, "Yes, they have all done well while you were away. A few times they had to stumble around in the dark holding the lantern to finish up the chores."

"Have you been trusting God?" he asked.

"Oh, yes," Lois answered, " 'cause sometimes we were afraid while you were gone."

After breakfast the following morning, Alvin lay a new doll in each of the girl's hands, and he gave Jimmy a new football. Bob and Dink's dolls both had blue eyes and blond hair like theirs. Lois' doll was a brunette like Lois. The dolls looked somewhat like the famous actress Shirley Temple, whose hair hung in ringlets all around her head. Their eyes closed when the dolls were laid down. They had tiny little white teeth. "I hope these dolls will take the place of the dolls you left behind in Oklahoma," he said. "If I had known how much you loved Joe, I would have let you bring him along."

"That's all right," Bob said, as she hugged her new doll. "God helped us find the doll without an arm in Shorty's bean field, and he let us keep it."

"You can't leave these dolls outside. They are made of pressed sawdust. If they get wet, they will soften and crumble. Don't ever take them outside. Always play with them inside the house. You are big girls now, almost too old for dolls, and these will possibly be the only dolls I will ever buy for you. Show your appreciation to God and to me by taking care of them, okay?"

"We will," each one promised.

Alvin kept his promise and took Mabel to Salem. The following afternoon, after they had gone shopping, a big truck pulled up beside their house. Two men carried in a new bedroom suit with a headboard, a tall chest of drawers, a wide vanity dresser with a huge round mirror, and a cute little stool to sit on while looking in the mirror. "It's sooo pretty," Lois said. She sat down and looked at herself. Then the three girls took turns sitting on the stool and gazing at themselves.

Questions for discussion:

1. What did Alvin love to do?
2. Why did Alvin go away to work?
3. What did he bring home?
4. Did the children work together while he was gone?
5. What did Mama get for a gift?
6. Who watched over the family while Alvin was gone?

These are Bob and Dink's Christmas dolls that Daddy brought when he came home after working in Los Angeles. The little cup was given to Mabel when her mother died in 1907. The lamp belonged to Mabel's papa. The two ice-cream dishes were Grandma Lou Hightower's. This photo was taken in April of 2017.

31 A Letter from Uncle Cornelius

But whoso hath this world's good, and sees his brother have need, and shuts up his bowels [of compassion] from him, how dwells the love of God in him?
1 John 3:17

As they were gathering in the living room one evening, Dink noticed a letter on Mama's lap. She hoped Mama would read it to them.

Alvin loved to sing, and before he had married, he had taught singing classes in the school houses which were used as community centers in those years long-ago. At times, he explained to the children how to read notes. If the children were in a singing mood, the family would sing many songs; however, tonight without singing, Daddy took a few moments encouraging his family to always trust in God. "God will certainly bless you as He blessed the Bible characters who trusted in Him," he said. "But if you allow others to destroy your faith in God, you will also make foolish decisions just as those Bible characters who turned away from God made unwise decisions. God has done many amazing things for our family just like He did for those who trusted Him

A Faithful Father

in Bible times. Children, there are going to be some changes in this home, but we can and must keep trusting in God. Mabel has a letter to read to you that will explain some of the changes."

Mama began reading the letter.

> "Dear Alvin,
>
> How are you? How is Mabel and the children? I trust all are well.
>
> We are well except for Grandma She is suffering much with the affliction on her face. She is in pain much of the time so she isn't able to get the boys up and ready for school. Therefore, I'm in trouble with the school authorities again as I was that time in Oklahoma. They are threatening to take the boys away from me and put them in a corrective institution. Also, Bill's friends aren't the best. I'm afraid he might get into serious trouble if I don't get him away from these friends.
>
> I was wondering if you and Mabel thought you might be able to keep them for a while? I know that's putting a lot on Mabel, but I have no one else to turn too. Maybe if you keep them during the remainder of this school term and during the summer, they will be more willing to attend classes and cooperate better with Grandma.
>
> I surely would appreciate your help. I can't be home and keep working to earn money to supply for them. Let me know what you think.
>
> Love, Cornelius

Alvin cleared his throat and said, "You children know that Aunt Montella died and Cornelius has had to raise his seven children alone. Grandma helps all she can, but she isn't well.

Mabel helped a lot when both our families lived in Oklahoma. We think we should help him again. Mabel has already written Cornelius telling him to send the boys and we will do the best we can for them.

"We told him that Mabel isn't very well and that the boys will have to help with the work. You children will also have to pitch in and help a little more and show the boys how to work together."

Dink kicked Bob gently. They smiled at each other and nodded in agreement. Now they would have someone else to play with.

Dad continued speaking, "You all can also help by being careful to obey the rules around here. What are some of the rules of this home?"

"We have to obey you and Mama," Lois said.

"Sure, but name some things you know to do without Mama or me reminding you?"

"We have to come to eat when Mama calls us," Jimmy said.

"Yes. No finishing the game, or the job and then come. Drop whatever you are doing and don't keep your mother waiting. She has worked hard to prepare the meal. Show her you appreciate it by coming while she is serving it."

"And we have to go to school and obey the teachers," Jimmy added.

"Yes. When you make problems for your teacher, you are in trouble with me. Always remember that," Daddy reminded them.

"We must do our chores without complaining," Bob said.

"And get up and be ready for school on time," Dink added.

"And comb your hair before going to school," Jim remarked to tease Dink about the day she forgot to comb her hair.

"I don't think we will have much trouble out of you all, because you are very good and obedient children," Daddy said.

"How will they get here?" Jim asked.

"They will come on the Greyhound bus. Mabel and I will pick them up in Albany."

"And when are they coming?" Dink asked excitedly. "I can hardly wait." Mabel caught Dink's eye. Dink thought Mama was thinking about the time when Tom and Dick had persuaded her to steal candy. Mabel said nothing. Dink was happy that Mama kept quiet about her secret.

"They will be here Monday morning. Uncle Cornelius won't have money to buy their tickets until he gets paid on Saturday. They will be riding on the bus all Saturday night, Sunday and Sunday night."

"Is Los Angeles that far away?" Dink asked. "Won't they be afraid on the bus by themselves?"

"When a person fails to do what he should do, he creates trouble for himself. That is happening to these boys. Because they did not obey their dad, Grandma, nor the school authorities, they will suffer the long trip alone and will have to be away from friends and their immediate family."

"I think Dick will cry having to leave Grandma and his daddy," Lois said.

"He probably will," Alvin said. "Poor little Dick will suffer because Bill did not obey authorities. Everyone has less trouble when they obey the rules of their authorities, even if they don't understand why they should. People also have additional trouble when they try to make life easier by not doing what they know they should do. Can you children always remember that?"

"Please try to remember to show the boys how a family works together. They have not lived in a home where people work together as we do," Mabel reminded them.

"Yes, that is right. Now let us pray and get to bed. We have a lot of things to do getting ready for your cousins. Mabel and I will go to the auction Friday evening and look for another bed and a chest of drawers," Alvin said.

"And we will need more chairs so they can be with us in family worship," Dink added.

"They can sit on the floor for worship like I did when we first moved here, but they will need chairs to sit a little higher at the table," Jimmy said. Everyone laughed.

After each one had prayed and told each other goodnight, Dink went bouncing up the stairs to get things prepared for her cousins' coming. At the top of the stairs the girls decided they would give one of their bedrooms to the younger boys, Tom, age ten and Dick, eight. Bill, who was thirteen, could share Jimmy's room, for he was almost as old as Jimmy.

They were up early the following morning moving Lois' things into the bedroom where Bob and Dink slept. To make room for Lois' things, Bob and Dink had to rearrange their playhouse, which was set up inside the huge closet. Jimmy had to clean his room and rearrange his clothes, too. He also cleaned out drawers so Bill would have a place for his belongings.

Questions for discussion:

1. Who was coming?
2. Why were the boys coming?
3. What were the children to do?
4. What were some rules of the home?
5. What adds trouble to anyone's life?
6. What makes life easier and better?

32 A Narrow Escape

The soul that sins, it shall die. The son shall not bear the iniquity of the father, neither shall the father the iniquity of the son. . . . But if the wicked shall turn from all the sins that he hath committed, and keep all my statues and do that which is lawful and right, he shall surely live, he shall not die. Ezekiel 18:20, 21

Jim and Bill picked up their lunch sacks and started for school. It was a little earlier than usual. Tom and Dick had also left early so they could play before the school bell rang. The girls were still at home getting dressed. As soon as Bill and Jimmy were a good way from home, Bill remarked excitedly, "Why you say, we mustn't go? No one will know we are gone until evening. Wow, a whole day without rain is a good day to travel. We might get halfway to California by evening."

"I don't want to go to California," Jim mumbled, as he followed Bill.

"But you said you would go with me," Bill replied.

"We can't get there in one day. Where will we sleep tonight? What will we eat for supper and tomorrow? I just want to go fishing, to just loaf around again. I'm so tired of going to school, chopping wood, feeding chickens and those old rabbits. I just need a day of rest."

"I really want to go see my Dad. I know it will get scary, and we just might have to be hungry a few days; but then we might not. Someone might feel sorry for us and buy us a hot meal, or we could steal bread and fruit along the way."

"Steal? No I wouldn't do that. That's not right. My Dad would really be disappointed if I stole."

"You're just afraid of your Dad, but I'm not; and I'm not afraid to steal when I'm hungry either. Even the Bible says it's all right to steal when you are hungry."

"It does not," Jimmy retorted.

"It sure does. Well, if we are not going to school, let's do something fun. I hid our fishing poles in the barn. I'm going back to find them," Bill said. Jimmy sat down behind a tree beside the road and waited. When Bill came back, they headed for the river.

They fished all morning but caught nothing. After eating the lunches that Mabel had packed for them to take to school, they lay down in the warm sand and both fell asleep.

When Bill awoke, he said, "Say, why don't we cross the river and see if the fish will bite better over there?"

"How long did we sleep? It's kind of late. I think it's about time we get home and do our chores. If we are late getting them done, we'll be in double trouble," Jimmy said.

"It's not late. Look the sun is high in the sky. Let's go across," Bill insisted.

"I don't want to go," Jimmy answered.

"You are such a *fraidy-cat*," Bill mocked. "Come on, and if you don't, then I'm going without you." And he took off toward the train bridge.

Jimmy looked at the sun then drew a clock in the sand to decide the time of day. If the shadow pointed north it was 12:00 o'clock. "It must be about 2:00," he murmured: "still early."

The train bridge was long and high. It went north and south over the North Santiam River. The boys were on the north side. While they were walking, they talked excitedly about the fish they might catch. When they were getting fairly close to the south bank, but still over deep water, Jimmy said. "Hey, I heard the train whistle, but it doesn't sound very loud. Hurry, Bill, and we can make it before the train gets here."

They ran until they were almost to the bank of the river. "We can jump down as soon as we get across the water," Jim called above the deafening noise as the train whistle blasted in their ears. "Hurry. I can feel the vibrating of the train already. It can't be far away."

"We have already passed the protective netting; we could jump," Bill said. In those days, when a train bridge spanned a great distance, there was a chance that the motion of the train and the great distance spanned could cause the bridge to sway. This had caused trains to come off the rails and plunge into rivers. To prevent this, there were protecting iron reinforcements along the center portion of the bridge.

"Lord, please save us. Have mercy on us, Lord. We won't make it, if you don't help," Jimmy prayed as he positioned himself to get off and down under the bridge. "Hurry, Bill," he shouted.

"I'm going as fast as I can," Bill called. He was already breathless.

"We've got to get off," Jimmy called. "We'll—get smashed—if—if the train comes around that curve; it'll be on us."

"But I can't swim in this raging current," Bill wailed.

"I can't either. Which is better; to drown or be chewed to pieces? I'm taking my chance in the water," Jimmy answered, and started climbing off the bridge.

"No, no," Bill cried, "You will drown."

"And you will, too. The train is on us! I can feel its heat!" Jimmy cried.

Jimmy wrapped his arms around a railroad tie not far from the rail that the speeding train would soon be on. He wondered if heat from the hot steel wheel would burn his arms or the vibration of the rushing train would knock him into the icy, raging water. There was no time to reconsider his moves. He had to get out of the way of that roaring train! He slid off the tract. He held his breath his eyes tightly closed and his jaws clinched.

Moments later, the train engine followed by many boxcars went racing over Jimmy as he hung suspended above the icy water. It didn't burned his arms. He was still dangling above the water, so he prayed again, "Please, dear God, keep my hands tight and my arm muscles strong. I can't do this without you. I can't possibly hold myself here more than a few minutes. It's sure death if my strength gives way!"

The train had passed. He was alive. While struggling to inch his way to the edge of the water so he could jump down, he called, "Bill, are you all right?"

"Yes, I'm down on the sand," Bill called up to Jim who was still dangling above the icy water.

Jim breathed a sigh of relief and struggled one inch more. He stopped to rest. Then he moved a few inches closer to the bank. He rested again, then moved on a bit closer. He begged God's help constantly, while struggling to keep from falling. Finally, the sand was below him! He turned loose and fell unto the soft sand. "Thank you, God, I'm on solid ground," he whispered.

A Faithful Father

As quickly as he had thanked God, he also realized how near he came to death. His anger at Bill returned. "Yeah, your great idea just about got us killed, that's what it did. Just think, we could be lost in that powerful current and our folks hunting everywhere for us, and then find us dead. My mama would die of grief if her only boy drowned— and Daddy would, too. And think how your dad would feel, if my dad called and told him that you were dead. I'm not following you again. Now let's go home."

Jimmy got up and started for home. It was a long way. They had to walk a good distance south to be able to climb up on to the high bridge. Then they had to walk back that distance, back across the river and then on home.

As they were walking back across the railroad bridge, Bill mumbled, "Sometimes I wish I could die. Life's been so miserable since Mama died. And now I can't be with Dad. I left all my friends in Los Angeles, and Uncle Alvin won't let us do anything, not even go to the movies."

"There aren't no movie houses around here anyway. We have to go all the way to Stayton, and that would take a lot of gasoline. Don't you like to play football, hide-and-seek and piggy wants a signal?"

"Well, a little bit; but when I was home, I went often to the movies 'cause Ellen is working in the ticket office and she got me in free."

"I'm sorry, Bill, about your mama, and all that, but there is a good supper waiting for us at home. Aren't you hungry?"

"Not really. I don't think Uncle Alvin likes me."

"Sure, he does. He treats you just like he does me. He works hard to buy our food and things we need. Doesn't that show that he loves you?"

"Maybe just because my Dad asked him to."

When Alvin came home from work, it was dark, and the boys were still doing chores. "Why aren't the chores done before now?" he asked Mabel.

"Jimmy and Bill didn't come in until about six-thirty. Bill said they went to the river after school," she answered.

Alvin turned to Lois, "Was Bill at school today?"

"No," she answered.

"Played hooky again. Did Jimmy go to school?"

"No one attends the school where he goes," Mabel replied.

"Now I've got something else to take care off," Alvin said. He sat down in his chair, sighed, picked up his Bible and began quickly turning pages.

A dark gray gloom hung over the family at supper that night. Jimmy's head hung over his plate. Bill was nervous and hardly ate anything. Mabel tried to be cheerful, but all the children kept their eyes on their plates. Daddy never mentioned the problem.

After the dishes were done, they gathered as usual for worship in the living room. They sang three songs rather mournfully and then Alvin read Ezekiel 14:12-23:

> *The word of the Lord came again to me, saying, Son of man, when the land sinneth against me by trespassing grievously, then will I stretch out mine hand . . . and will send famine upon it, . . . Though these three men, Noah, Daniel, and Job be in it, . . . they shall deliver neither son nor daughter; they shall but deliver their own souls by their righteousness. . . . Yet, behold, therein shall be left a remnant . . . and ye shall know that I have not done without cause all that I have done in it, saith the Lord God.*
>
> Another scripture that goes with this lesson is found Ezekiel 18:20-21. It tells us, *'The soul that*

sins it shall die. The son shall not bear the iniquity of the father, neither shall the father the iniquity of the son. . . . But if the wicked shall turn from all the sins that he hath committed, and keep all my statues and do that which is lawful and right, he shall surely live, he shall not die.'

Alvin laid his Bible on his lap, took off his glasses, and said, "When the people sinned, God caused a famine and they had no food. Although great righteous men such as Noah, Daniel and Job were in the city, they could not save it from the discipline it deserved. Neither could they save their own children from suffering during the famine. These scriptures show four important things.

"First, it shows that there are consequences for sinful actions, whether it is an individual, a family, or a nation.

"Second, it shows that every person will receive what is due to him according to his actions.

"Third, it shows that a righteous parent cannot deliver a disobedient child from God's judgement.

"The fourth thing it tells is that every person must deliver himself by repenting and doing right, and then he will understand that God's disciplines are for good.

"Children, always remember that serving God is best. He blesses those who honor Him, whether you are a parent or a child. God always allows those who have sinned to come back to him and live. Both of these scriptures give the sinner a chance to change and live. Always remember that, but also remember there are penalties to pay if we keep on sinning. Jimmy and Bill, remember what I just read, and I will talk to you after the others are gone to bed."

Each one prayed, said goodnight, and the other children went upstairs.

They could hear Daddy talking to Jimmy and Bill.

Questions for discussion:

1. What sins did Jim and Bill commit?
2. Tell how they were almost killed?
3. In the Bible, what happened to the nation that was sinful?
4. Could Noah, Daniel or Job save the nation?
5. What act could save the nation?
6. Is each person responsible for his own sins?
7. Does God give people an opportunity to change?

33 Yellow Jackets at War

For nothing is secret that shall not be made manifest: neither anything hid that shall not be made known and come abroad. Luke 8:17

Mrs. Schofield finished writing the new spelling words on the chalkboard, then she turned to the class and said, "Students, you may stand and go in single file out for recess. Enjoy the beautiful sunshine, but remember that going off the school ground is not allowed unless you have written permission."

The students filed out. Each one was excited to play in the sunshine, because sunny days were rare during Oregon's winters. Lois, Roberta and Dink ran for the swings. Dink got the first one. Roberta and Lois each got one, but Roberta, being always polite, let Glenda have her swing. One of the boys snatched the other swing.

Several girls in the upper grades had boyfriends; so on the playground south of the school building, they started a game called *last couple out*. Some younger children were playing tag. A group of girls were jumping rope in the play shed. Some boys were throwing a ball and catching it; others were playing tackle football. While most of the children were playing, Raymond, Carl, Ralph, Evert and Tom headed for the woods behind the school. "The woods are off limits," Glenda called, when she noticed her little brother, Dean, running after the older boys.

"I won't go across the fence," he called back to her. "I just want to see the beehive that Ralph found."

"You mean the yellow jacket hive?" Ralph corrected him. As the boys neared the fence, Ralph said, "Look, it's right over there." He pointed toward a round, gray mass with a tiny hole in the upper center.

"Come over here, where the fence is broken down. We can get across easily," Raymond called. The boys followed him.

"We shouldn't go off the school yard," Dean said.

"Don't be a sissy. No one will know. We won't go far," Raymond said, reproaching Dean. "Come on or you can't see the yellow jackets going in and out," Ralph insisted.

When the boys got near the hive, Tom remarked, "No bees are coming in or going out."

"Remember, these are yellow jackets, not bees," Ralph corrected Tom.

"They must be asleep. We'll have to wake them up," Evert said. He found a long stick and tapped on the hive. A few yellow jackets came out.

"Let's throw rocks and see if we can get more action," Raymond suggested. The boys backed away, and first one then another started throwing rocks. Soon, yellow jackets were buzzing all around the hive. The boys laughed and threw more rocks.

"I'm getting out of here!" Dean shouted, and he started running toward the school building.

"Scaredy-cat," the boys called in unison as they watched Dean running away. When they turned back toward the hive, hundreds of yellow jackets were billowing out. The boys ran in all directions out over the school yard with yellow jackets flying after them.

The boys were dodging and swatting as more yellow jackets came swarming out of the hive. "Ouch, one just stung me," Evert yelled.

"These guys are mad as hornets," called Raymond. "Hey, three got me." The majority of the yellow jackets were staying together and following Raymond, who was headed toward the back door of the school.

The back door was very near the swings. Roberta, who was standing beside the swings, saw Raymond running and the cloud of yellow jackets following him. She screamed, "A swarm of bees is coming! Run!" She ran into the back door of the school. By now Mrs. Schofield and Mrs. Wheeler were at the door fighting back yellow jackets as the students came running in.

Glenda jumped off and ran inside when she saw the yellow jackets chasing her brother, Dean. Wilma and Dink were swinging together. Dink was facing the swarm of yellow jackets and yelled, "Everybody jump! The bees are coming toward us."

"I can't jump, I'm too high," Lois cried. Just then a yellow jacket stung her on the hand. She screamed and swatted the insect. Another stung her arm. She was hanging onto the swing with one hand and swatting yellow jackets with the other.

When the swing that Dink and Wilma were in came down low, Dink jumped and tumbled onto the ground. She jumped up quickly and shouted again, "Jump everybody! Jump out of the swings. The yellow jackets will sting you."

"They are all over me," Lois yelled.

"Jump anyway!" Dink called again.

"I can't. I can't see. The bees are on my eyes."

Amid the numerous yellow jackets, Wilma waited until the swing was again close to the ground, then she jumped. The swing caught her foot. To protect herself, Wilma threw out both hands. Dink ran to help her. Wilma landed on her arms before Dink caught her. Both arms broke on impact and her face smashed into the dirt. Slapping yellow jackets and screaming loudly, Dink helped Wilma get up. Wilma's arms hung limp like two rags as she ran crying into the schoolhouse door, the angry yellow jackets clinging to her back.

Dink ran back to help Lois. To keep from falling, Lois had both arms around the chains that held the swing, and with her hands was swatting the stinging beasts. Yellow jackets were hanging all over Lois, on her legs, her face, her back and tangled in her hair. Dink grabbed the swing chain to stop the swing. Lois jumped off. Dink could hear the buzzing of angry yellow jackets tangled in Lois' long hair. Lois, already nearly blind from her swollen eyes, straggled toward the school building. Dink followed her, slapping the yellow jackets off Lois and herself.

Mrs. Wheeler took Lois into the kitchen and killed the remaining yellow jackets. Then she combed the dead ones out of Lois' long hair. "Yellow jackets are more aggressive than other stinging insects such as wasps, hornets, mud daubers or bees," Mrs. Wheeler told them. "Also, yellow jackets can both sting and bite. Since they don't lose their stinger, the same insect can sting many times."

By now, Lois' face was so puffy she was not recognizable. Her arms, legs and body were swollen, making her look very fat.

Mrs. Schofield put Lois and Wilma into her car and drove them to their homes.

Just before school was dismissed for the evening, Mrs. Schofield took her place in front of all the students attending the North Santiam School. "A very serious thing has happened today," she said. "Lois Hightower is very near death. We hope and pray that God will relieve her body of this poison and the severe

A Faithful Father

suffering and that he will spare her life. Wilma Glidewell is also suffering. She is at the hospital getting casts on her two broken arms. For many weeks Wilma will be unable to feed herself, to put on her clothes, to comb her hair or brush her teeth, or even scratch her nose." Everyone laughed. "Yes, it sounds funny, but it is not funny. It is very serious—, and it could have been avoided. Some boys disobeyed and went off the school grounds, and I know who they are. I know you did not know these terrible things would happen if you angered the yellow jackets. However, you see what has happened and that two of your fellow students are suffering intensely. I will bring this problem before the school board and will follow their recommendation as to what will be done to the boys who caused this problem. You are all dismissed."

Dink and Bob ran home to see about Lois. When they got home, Lois was asleep in Mama's bed downstairs. "Is she going to live?" Bob asked.

"She looks like a *blowed* up balloon," Dink whispered. "And it makes me so mad. Just for fun, those boys stirred up the yellow jackets, and look what happened. Gloria, Glena, Mary, Dean and lots of others went home sick from stings. I hope they really feel horrible and think long and hard about the results of their actions."

"Yes, they should," Mabel agreed. "We all should think about the consequences of our actions and before doing something think how it might affect us or someone else.

Tom was also hurting from his stings, but mostly, he was hurting inside, wondering if Uncle Alvin might send him back to Los Angeles? He loved living in Oregon.

That night, after family worship, the family gathered around Mama's bed and prayed for Lois. All through the night, whenever Dink awoke, she could hear either Mama or Daddy praying. She knew they were praying for Lois.

The following morning Lois was asleep when the girls came down, but she still looked much like a balloon. For many days, she missed school because she was very sick.

Wilma stayed home almost a month. Mrs. Schofield sent books and lessons home for Wilma by her older brother, Ralph.

Questions for discussion:

1. Where were the children to play?
2. Did the boys think no one would know?
3. Were they able to keep it a secret?
4. Should we think how our actions will affect others?
5. Should the boys apologize for causing so much pain?
6. Does God know everything?

34 When Jimmy Ran Away

And if it seems evil unto you to serve the Lord, choose ye this day whom ye will serve but as for me and my house we will serve the Lord. Joshua 24:15

Jimmy and Bill would sometimes skip school and play during school hours down by the river. Then they would show up at home at the usual evening chore time. One day, when they skipped school, Tom got very angry at them, possibly because they would not let him go along. They came home at the usual time, went right to work chopping wood, feeding the chickens, rabbits and pigs, and no one acted like they knew the boys had not gone to school that day. However, Tom tattled on them for vengeance. After supper, Dad scolded them even more severely than he had done at other times when they had not gone to school. This made both boys so angry that they planned another escapade.

Weeks later, when all the children left for school, Bill and Jimmy took off hitchhiking to Los Angeles, California where Bill's dad lived. That was 900 miles away. It was November. The weather was cold and rainy that day as they walked down the road hoping for a ride. The longer they walked, the more miserable they felt. By early afternoon, Jimmy was missing those delicious meals that he was accustomed to every day and wishing for his warm bed and security for the night, so he persuaded Bill that a spanking was better than staying all night outside in the cold. They chose the spanking and came home.

In the spring, when the weather warmed up, the two boys started again on the 900-mile trip to California. When evening came, they did not return home.

Tom, Dick and the girls had to chop and carry in the wood and the other chores that Bill and Jim usually did. Quietness, like icy hands of death, hung over the family that night. They prepared supper without the usual chattering about the day's happenings. They ate in silence without Dad's childhood stories that usually accompanied meals. Dink noticed Lois sniffing and wiping an occasional tear. Mama was stirring her fork in her food but not eating.

After the kitchen was cleaned, Dad called everyone to gather around for the nightly family worship. Only this night they did not sing, instead, Dad talked a long time about the structure of a home and the importance of each one doing his part to make it happy. Then he said, "You all know that Bill and Jim are gone again. You know that I have forgiven them many times for skipping classes, and you also know that I have been good to both boys. I have given them plenty of food, clothes, a good home, and a warm bed. All I asked of them and of you is that you cooperate with the work that is needed to keep our home running smoothly, and that you also obey the rules your mother and I have made for our home. These rules are only for your good. Let's name some of the rules. Who can tell me one?"

No one wanted to speak.

After a long silence, Lois said, "Go to school and do our homework."

A Faithful Father

Tom said, "Don't use bad words."

Dink said, "Obey your mother and father."

Bob said, "Just be good. That covers every rule."

Then Dad spoke again, "I think you all know the rules. When you obey the rules of this home you can share the food and comforts of this home. Anytime either of you do not want to stay here, you have the privilege to leave and find somewhere else to live. We are doing the best we can for you.

"Bill and Jimmy have chosen to leave. Many times they have broken the rules by not attending school. One thing that you can do is to leave and then come back when things get tough. Once you make your choice to make your home somewhere else, this is no longer your home. You are welcome to come home for visits, but you must return to your residence in that other place."

Dink could hardly believe her ears. Did he really mean that Jim, her big brother, her idol, could not be a part of their family now? She wanted to scream, "You can't do that to my Jimmy."

Then Dad turned to Mom and said very seriously, "Get their clothes and put them in separate boxes. We will set them on the porch in case they want them." Mom got up, tears streaming down her face and went toward the stairway door.

"I don't feel like walking upstairs. Lois, will you please go get the boys' clothes?" Mama said.

Lois got up and obediently went upstairs. Dink noticed Lois' eyes were red and her face was also wet. Mama slipped into the kitchen. Dink looked at Bob, and she was wiping her face on her sleeve. Dink was too shocked to cry. She couldn't believe what was happening. Finally, she mustered up enough courage to say, "Can't Jim live here anymore, Daddy?"

"He will have to decide that," Daddy answered. "If he is willing to obey the rules, we will figure out a way that he can stay. One of the rules is, go to school and come directly home. He has broken that rule many, many times, and it is now nine o'clock, and he hasn't come in yet."

By this time, Lois had returned with her arms full of clothes. There were Jim's bib overalls and striped polo shirt that he wore the day the school pictures were made and his brown sweater he wore for his eighth-grade graduation. She piled them on the kitchen table, and from where Dink sat, she saw Mama bury her face in a shirt and sob. Then she mechanically began folding and placing Jimmy's clothes into a big box. When she had finished with Jim's, she reached for another box, and she did the same with the few clothes that Bill had.

The family knelt, Dad prayed first, then each one prayed as they did every night. But this time, everyone prayed for Jim and Bill to be good and to come home soon.

"Now you all go to bed," Dad said, "and don't a one of you come down if Jim and Bill do come in.

The children slipped upstairs with heads drooping like five whipped puppies. Bob, the most obedient, went first, then Lois, Tom, Dick and then Dink stomping her feet on every step as soon as she was out of her Daddy's sight. At the top of the stairs they held a counsel. (That is all except Lois; she went to her bed and knelt down.) The rest of the children decided that they would take turns standing guard to see if Jim and Bill came home and if they chose to stay. No one could wait until morning to know if they were losing their brothers or not.

They could see the road from the north window in Bill and Jim's bedroom. Lying on their stomachs across Jim's bed with eyes glued on the road, they watched and hoped. An hour or so later, they saw a car stop in front of the house. Jim and Bill got out. Dink tiptoed quietly down to stand guard at the bottom of the stairs to listen through the crack in the door.

After Jim and Bill came in, Roberta and Tom joined her at the bottom of the stairs; and soon Lois, and Dick also came down.

Dad told the boys just what he had said during worship that evening. When he finished, he asked, "Now boys what is your decision?"

The children all held their breath as they listened for the boys' decision. After what seemed like a long, long time, Bill spoke. "I'm sorry Uncle Alvin. It's all my fault. I persuaded Jim to go with me to see my daddy. I won't do it anymore. I promise."

"If you won't, then you may stay. But remember, Bill, if you leave again without permission, you cannot come back. I will send you back to your father, and the juvenile authorities will pick you up."

"I promise to be good. Please let me stay," Bill pleaded.

Then Dad turned to Jim and asked, "Are you willing to obey the rules of this home?"

"I will," Jim promised his voice trembling.

"Then you can stay, so long as you cooperate."

The children, standing breathless at the bottom of the stairs, relaxed, hugged each other and as quickly and quietly as possible, snuck into their beds. When scarcely under the covers, they heard Daddy helping the boys carry their boxes of clothes up into Jim's room. Each one pretended to be asleep when Dad peeked in to check on them.

Questions for discussion:

1. In what ways did Jim and Bill disobey?
2. Was this the first time they skipped school?
3. Why did the boys return the first time they left to go to Los Angeles?
4. What did Dad say each child should do?
5. What choice did Jim and Bill have to make?
6. Did they make the right choice?

Dink in the woods.

35 A Happy Daddy

The law of [God's] mouth is better unto me than thousands of gold and silver. Psalms 119:72

Dink noticed that her daddy had been whistling, singing and laughing more lately. She was thinking every night in family worship that he would share some exciting news. Were his brothers, Jim and Cornelius, and Grandma going to also move to Oregon? She knew Daddy had missed his family greatly. Most of their lives they had lived close together and had seen each other every few days. Had he been promised a new job with good pay? Was Mama to have a new baby, maybe twins? Several times in the last few weeks, Mama and Daddy had driven into town by themselves. What were they doing on these secret missions? Every evening when the family came together for family worship she expected her Daddy to reveal the secret that was making him so happy.

The North Santiam School that the children attended was just around the bend on a gravel road from the old farmhouse they were renting, so the children walked home for lunch. Dick and Dink often raced each other, but Bob only raced sometimes.

Lois didn't like to run, and Tom often tripped when he ran; so he preferred to walk with Lois. Mama always had a hot lunch waiting for them.

One day, when they were returning to school, Raymond came down the road to walk beside Dink. In a few minutes, Carl and Dereck came also and began calling, "sweethearts, sweethearts," to Dink and Raymond. Dink acted as if she would hit them, so they ran away as she chased them. Soon they were back, and she chased them off again. The boys came back the third time after they had entered the school yard, and Dink again began chasing Carl. With Dink close behind him, Carl dashed into the open school house and slammed the door. Dink threw out her hand to keep the door from hitting her face. Her hand crashed through the glass pane of the door.

Mrs. Schofield came quickly. She carefully removed Charlotte's hand from the jagged glass protruding from the window. She picked pieces of glass out of the gash with her tweezers, washed and bandaged Dink's hand. Then she sent Lois to walk home with her.

When Mama unwrapped Dink's hand and saw the long cut, she gasped. Then holding Dink's hand firmly in hers, she began praying. Praying was Mama's first response when anyone got hurt. Dink stopped trembling when she began praying. It was weeks before Dink could do many chores around the house. The cut left a long, but almost invisible, scar on her left hand.

When Daddy came home and sat down in his chair, Mabel took Dink to his chair, unwrapped her hand and showed it to him. Then she told him what happened. "Well, you should get a spanking for such wild behavior at school. Haven't I told you to not run in places where you might get hurt or might hurt someone else?"

"Yes," Dink answered, with her head hanging low.

"Then why did you disobey?"

"At that moment, I forgot."

"I am sorry you forgot and got hurt," he said, and drew Dink down onto his lap. Then hugging her he said, "You know what? When you hurt, I hurt, but you must be more careful to remember, or next time I will give you something that will help you to remember." Dink nodded and put her arms around her dear daddy and hugged him. He smiled and added, "And guess what's going to happen tonight?" Dink shrugged her shoulders. "I read in the newspaper that tonight we should be able to see a shower of meteors if it isn't too cloudy. That is why I came home early tonight."

"What are meteors?" Dink asked. Are they those things we put money in when we park on the street in Salem? What kind of shower would that be?"

"Oh, Dink," Jimmy said, and bowed over laughing.

"Is that when stars fall like it says in the Bible?" Lois asked.

"In Revelations?" he asked.

"I guess," she answered.

"Most people think of meteors as stars. They are heavenly bodies. However, in Revelations when it speaks of stars it is referring to pastors of church congregations or ministers of the Gospel, not stars that we see in the sky."

"In one place I read that one third of the stars fell. Does that mean that many pastors fell from God's grace?" Lois questioned.

"Yes, at one time in the history of the church some very convincing men persuaded many pastors to stop preaching the doctrines that Christ taught. When they began teaching false doctrines, their lights went out, and they fell from the holy place where God had placed them."

"What did the people do when their preachers started teaching false doctrines?" Lois asked.

"The changes came so slowly that many people did not recognize the wrong and they accepted it. Then they also became deceived and lost God's sweet approval on their lives. Are all you children listening?" Alvin asked in a loud voice. Bob was already listening. Jimmy laid down the book he was reading. The other boys were outside playing. "It is very important that you hear what I'm going to say. Be very careful through life that when you hear or see changes in the church that you study your Bible and see if the changes are in agreement with God's Word. When changes come a little at a time or we are taught wrong by someone we trust, it is very easy to follow the group and lose God's approval. Keeping your relationship with Christ is the most important thing you can do. It is more important than men's admiration, money, or anything else in life. Children, guard sincerely your relationship with Christ."

"Are we gonna miss seeing the stars falling?" Dink interrupted.

Jimmy laughed again at Dinks senseless questioned. "We can't see the stars until after dark. It's not dark yet."

"I think we have time to eat, if Mabel has it ready?" Alvin said. "Then we will go outside and be ready when darkness settles."

"It's ready," Mabel responded, as she set a pan of hot biscuits on the table beside a skillet full of Spanish rice and a bowl of home-canned green beans.

They quickly gathered around the table. Alvin thanked God for the food and as usual, he asked God to bless the hands that prepared it. While they were eating, Alvin reached into his shirt pocket and pulled out a sheet of paper. He opened it and laid it flat on the table beside Mama's plate. She looked at it and smiled. Alvin smiled back, then he said, "When I was at Mr. Comstock's today, he gave me the contract on our new farm."

"What???" the children asked all at the same time. "Did you buy a farm?"

"Yes, Mabel and I have been looking at land and talking with Mr. Comstock for some time. We found a place in Marion that we both like and gave him the down payment last week. Today we received the legal papers."

Dink jumped up, ran around the table and hugged her daddy. Lois did, too.

"Mr. Comstock made arrangements for us to pay a payment once a year at the end of harvest. We have already saved enough for the down payment and to build a little house, so I'm sure we will be able to save for the payments. It's my lifetime dream come true!" he said, while laughing. He leaned back in his chair and stretched out his arms in a relaxed position. "We did it! Yes, we did! Our dream has come true because we obeyed and trusted God, and we all worked together."

"Wow! We have our own farm in the Willamette Valley," Jimmy said, with a big smile.

"Won't Daddy and Uncle Jim be excited to hear about it," Bill said.

"Uncle Jim and Aunt Mae are also thinking of buying a farm up here," Tom interjected.

"Yeah, really," Bill agreed.

"Land boarding ours is for sale; maybe he could buy it. He probably has money saved, with no children, a good job, and Mae teaching school. Mabel, why don't you write and tell them."

"Let me know the price and I will do that," Mabel answered.

"And Grandma will come, too?" Lois asked.

"If they come, Grandma will come, too. She lives with them now since she isn't well. We will need to keep working together until we get all the payments made," Mabel said.

"When will we build a house on it?" Bob asked.

"Mabel and I are going over tomorrow to decide on the place to build our house. It is a forest right now, but I will hire a bulldozer to clear it for us. Now let's get outside and see the fireworks that God has prepared for us." They put on their sweaters, while Jimmy and Bill brought a tarp from the woodshed. Daddy carried out a chair for Mama. Everyone else either sat or laid on the tarp to look up at the stars. "There is the Big Dipper and the Little Dipper," Lois said.

"I don't see a dipper in the sky," Dink complained.

"Over there is the bear," Mama pointed.

"Where is a bear?" Dink asked.

Just then, a little white streak flew through the air. "There goes a falling star!" Bob shouted excitedly. "Did you see it Dink?"

"That's not a falling star. That's just a fire fly, like we had in Oklahoma."

"No, Dink, that is a meteor falling into Earth's atmosphere. It is far, far away," Daddy said.

"There's another one and another," Lois cried. "They are falling all over the sky."

They watched silently for a good while as a continuing shower of meteors kept falling. Finally Dink asked, "Daddy, will there be any stars left in the sky?"

"Oh, yes, honey. God made plenty of stars, so we will have stars until the end of the world."

It was late that night after prayer when they finally crawled upstairs and fell into dreamland. Jimmy, Lois, Bob and Dink were dreaming of their own farm. Dick, Tom, and Bill were dreaming of their Daddy, Grandma and Uncle Jim moving to Oregon.

Questions for discussion:

1. How was Alvin feeling?
2. How did Dink get her hand cut?
3. What did Dink forget?
4. What handiwork of God did they watch?
5. What dream had come true?
6. Why had their dream come true?
7. Do you think Grandma and Alvin's brothers will move to Oregon?

Happy Daddy by a big tree on the farm.

About the Author

Charlotte's ability to write comes from the Master Author, God. Born dyslectic, she contributes her ability to do well in school to her siblings and her mother reading to her, and to having learned in Family Worship the discipline of listening prudently. Growing up on a farm has given her a lifelong love for plants, animals and everything pertaining to country life. She is a first-rate gardener.

Charlotte dedicated her life to serve God at a young age and has become a woman of prayer and solid faith. Her life-long vocation has been assisting others in obtaining a relationship with Christ. Charlotte's life has been relentlessly eventful: teaching, editing a children's Sunday school magazine, publishing articles for Christian families and serving years as a missionary in Mexico.

Her life has been filled with extraordinary experiences of which she writes in a simple manner that interests both adults and children. God has caused her modest efforts to bless people in countries around the world.

My Prayer
Psalms 71:17, 18

Oh God, thou hast taught me from my youth: hitherto have I declared thy wondrous works. Now also when I am old and grayheaded, O God, forsake me not until I have shewed thy strength unto this generation and thy power to everyone that is to come.

**Amen,
Charlotte**

About the Book

A *Faithful* Father is the true story of a family who, during the Great Depression and the Dust Bowl years loses everything except their faith and the fathers 1926 Reo car. Without a home for his family of six, the father accepts an offer to live with the owner and share-crop his farm. After struggling four more years during the drought, he makes his car into a pickup, leaves the farm and uses it to make a living until he is offered an opportunity in Oregon.

By trusting in God and working together for three years, the family purchases a farm in Oregon's lush Willamette Valley.

You will laugh and cry as you relive the sad and humorous experiences of this family.

Questions for discussion at the end of each chapter make it useful as a family or class devotional book.

CPSIA information can be obtained
at www.ICGtesting.com
Printed in the USA
FFOW05n1920230517